# 共和国七十年<sup>瞬间</sup>

## 70 YEARS OF THE PEOPLE'S REPUBLIC

庆祝中华人民共和国成立七十周年

The 70th Anniversary of the Founding of
The People's Republic of China

蒋永清 撰文
JIANG YONGQING

中国画报出版社·北京
China Pictorial Press·Beijing

图书在版编目（ＣＩＰ）数据

共和国七十年瞬间：汉英对照 / 蒋永清撰文；钟
丽莎译 . -- 北京：中国画报出版社，2019.9
　ISBN 978-7-5146-1793-1

　Ⅰ . ①共… Ⅱ . ①蒋… ②钟… Ⅲ . ①社会主义建设
成就 – 中国 – 画册 Ⅳ . ① D619-64

中国版本图书馆 CIP 数据核字 (2019) 第 183055 号


共和国七十年瞬间

蒋永清 撰文　钟丽莎 译

出 版 人：于九涛
策划编辑：于九涛
项目统筹：方允仲
责任编辑：刘晓雪
图片编辑：刘晓雪
英文编辑：叶淑君
英文改稿：迈克尔·杰弗里·默里
英文定稿：王国振　陈 旭
设　　计：郑建军
内文排版：李晓然
责任印制：焦 洋

出版发行：中国画报出版社
地　　址：中国北京市海淀区车公庄西路 33 号 邮编：100048
发 行 部：010-68469781 010-68414683（传真）
总编室兼传真：010-88417359　版权部：010-88417359

开　　本：16 开（889mm x 1194mm）
印　　张：17.25
字　　数：200 千字
版　　次：2019 年 9 月第 1 版 2019 年 9 月第 1 次印刷
印　　刷：北京汇瑞嘉合文化发展有限公司
书　　号：ISBN 978-7-5146-1793-1
定　　价：298.00 元

# 前言

1949 年 10 月 1 日，毛泽东 (1893—1976) 在天安门城楼上向全世界庄严宣告中华人民共和国成立，从此，中国进入了一个全新的时代。70 年披荆斩棘，70 年风雨兼程。中华人民共和国成立以来的 70 年，是不断创造伟大奇迹、彻底改变中华民族前途命运的 70 年。

70 年来，共和国在中国共产党坚强领导下，战胜各种艰难险阻，谱写了波澜壮阔的社会主义革命、建设、改革的壮丽诗篇，探索出古老文明走向现代化的发展道路，极大改善了中国人民的生活，极大提升了中国的国际地位和影响力。

70 年来，一个个奇迹极大改变了中国的面貌：经济上，我国国内生产总值在 2018 年首次突破 90 万亿元，稳居世界第二位；民生上，中国建成了世界上规模最大、覆盖人口最多的社会保障体系；科技上，从"两弹一星"、超级杂交水稻，到如今的云计算、人工智能等新技术发展，无不见证中国科技发展的突飞猛进；制度上，社会主义市场经济体制、"一国两制"等制度创新，为人类制度文明发展作出了独特贡献……70 年的奇迹昭示：只有社会主义才能救中国，只有中国特色社会主义才能发展中国，只有坚持和发展中国特色社会主义才能实现中华民族的伟大复兴。

70 年来，无数摄影师用手中的相机记录了共和国的沧桑巨变。这些难忘时刻和鲜活瞬间凝结成影像，形成一部珍贵的"国家记忆"。

"无限的过去都以现在为归宿，无限的未来都以现在为渊源。"每张照片都是一段历史，请跟随镜头回望来时路。

# PREFACE

On October 1, 1949, Mao Zedong (1893-1976) solemnly declared the founding of the People's Republic of China (PRC) to the whole world while standing on the Tian'anmen Rostrum in Beijing. Seventy years have passed and China is now in the midst of an exciting new era. Numerous facts show how these past 70 years have seen the PRC work wonders in totally altering the face of the Chinese nation.

Over this period, under the strong leadership of the Communist Party of China (CPC), the PRC has overcome all kinds of difficulties and obstacles, and composed magnificent poems of socialist revolution, socialist construction and reform and opening-up. Over that time, this ancient civilization has embarked on the road to full modernization, greatly improved the lives of its people, and greatly enhanced China's international status and influence.

Over this period, China has worked one miracle after another. Economically, its GDP surpassed 90 trillion Yuan for the first time in 2018, ranking second in the world. In regard to people's livelihood, it has built the world's largest social security system covering the largest population in the world. In science and technology, moving from the initial period of the "two bombs and one satellite" and creation of super hybrid rice helping to feed a growing world population to the current era of "cloud computing" and "artificial intelligence", all these developments bear witness to the giant leaps and bounds China has experienced in joining the world leaders in these fields. Institutionally, China has introduced the socialist market economic system and the policy of "one country, two systems", making unique contribution to the development of human institutional civilization. The many miracles it has created over the past seven decades clearly show that only socialism can save China, only by upholding socialism with Chinese characteristics can China develop, and only by adhering to and developing socialism with Chinese characteristics can China realize the great rejuvenation of the Chinese nation.

Over the past 70 years, a great number of photographers have recorded the vicissitudes of the People's Republic through their lens. These unforgettable vivid moments combine to form a precious "national memory".

"The infinite past is based on the present, and the infinite future is based on the present." Each photo in 70 Years of the People's Republic forms a part of history, creating an invaluable research tool.

# 目录
# CONTENTS

# 第一章 站起来
## Chapter I Chinese Nation Stands Up

中华人民共和国成立后，中国共产党带领人民迅速医治战争创伤、恢复国民经济，创造性地完成了由新民主主义向社会主义的转变。社会主义基本制度在中国的确立，为新中国的全面建设奠定了根本政治基础和制度保障。

针对如何建设适合中国国情的社会主义这个重大课题，党领导人民进行了艰苦探索。在不长的时间里，我国社会就发生了翻天覆地的变化，建立起独立的比较完整的工业体系和国民经济体系，独立研制出"两弹一星"，成为世界上有重要影响力的大国，积累起在中国这样一个社会生产力水平十分落后的东方大国进行社会主义建设的重要经验。

中华人民共和国的诞生、社会主义基本制度的确立和社会主义建设的全面展开，实现了中华民族由"积贫积弱"到站起来的伟大飞跃。

Right after the founding of the PRC in 1949, the CPC led the Chinese people to quickly heal the wounds of war, restore the national economy, and creatively complete the transformation from the new democratic revolution to a socialist one. The establishment of the basic socialist system in the People's Republic has laid a fundamental political prerequisite and institutional foundation for all the development and progress made by contemporary China.

In order to build socialism suitable for China's national conditions, the CPC has led the Chinese people through arduous theoretical and practcal explorations. In a short time, Chinese society has undergone tremendous changes, with the establishment of an independent and relatively complete industrial system and national economic system. "Two bombs [atomic and hydrogen] and one [space] satellite" were independently developed, turning China into a major influential country in the world. During the period, it accumulated important experience in socialist construction in a country that had previously had a very backward level of social productivity.

The birth of the PRC and the establishment of the basic socialist system and the comprehensive development of socialist construction combined to make it possible for the Chinese nation, formerly infamous in the West as the "sick man of East Asia", to stand up in the world.

1949 年 10 月 1 日，中华人民共和国开国大典在北京天安门广场隆重举行。图为董希文创作的油画作品《开国大典》（靳尚谊摹本）

On October 1, 1949, the Founding Ceremony of the People's Republic of China was held with great solemnity in Tian'anmen Square, Beijing. The picture shows Dong Xiwen's oil painting *The Founding Ceremony* - facsimile by Jin Shangyi.

**...*1950*...**

1950 年，我国颁布了第一部法律《中华人民共和国婚姻法》，实行男女婚姻自由、一夫一妻、男女权利平等、保护妇女和子女合法利益的新民主主义婚姻制度。图为 1952 年 11 月 9 日，湖南省醴陵县白兔潭村农民在区政府登记结婚，司法干部把结婚证书递给他们

The PRC promulgated its first law in 1950, the Marriage Law, implementing a new democratic system highlighting freedom of marriage between men and women, monogamy, equality of rights between the two sexes, and protection of the legitimate interests of women and children. This picture was taken on November 9, 1952, when peasants of Baitutan Village in Liling County, Hunan Province, registered for marriage with the district government, and received their marriage certificates from judicial workers.

1950 年 6 月 28 日，中央人民政府委员会通过了《中华人民共和国土地改革法》。这部法律废除了封建土地所有制，实行了农民阶级的土地所有制，使广大农民成为土地的主人。图为北京市郊区土地改革时农民在丈量土地的情形

On June 28, 1950, the Central People's Government Committee passed the Land Reform Law of the People's Republic of China. It abolished feudal land ownership and implemented the land ownership rights of the peasant class, ensuring peasants the masters of the land. The picture shows peasants measuring land as part of the land reform process in the suburbs of Beijing.

*··· 1950 ···*

1950 年 10 月 14 日，政务院发布《关于治理淮河的决定》，这是新中国水利建设事业的第一个大工程。70 年来，国家投入上万亿元开展大规模水利建设，一项项水利重点工程成为促进国家协调可持续发展的重要举措。图为治理淮河的第二期工程中，民工在河南省泌阳县板桥水库工地施工。

On October 14, 1950, the Government Administration Council of the Central People's Government (replaced by the State Council in 1954) issued the Decision on Harnessing the Huai River, which was the first major project of water conservancy construction in the PRC. In the past 70 years, the State has invested trillion of Yuan to carry out large-scale water conservancy construction for the coordinated and sustainable development of the national economy. The picture shows the Banqiao Reservoir construction project in Biyang County, Henan Province, during the second phase of the Huai River harnessing project.

### ··· *1950* ···

1950 年 10 月上旬，中共中央作出抗美援朝、保家卫国的
战略决策。图为 1950 年 10 月 19 日，中国人民志愿军雄起起、
气昂昂跨过鸭绿江，和朝鲜人民一道共同抗击侵略者

In early October 1950, the CPC Central Committee decided to aid the
DPRK in its effort to resist US aggression on the Korean Peninsula
and to protect China. The picture shows the Chinese People's
Volunteer Army crossing the Yalu River on October 19, 1950, to join
the Korean people in their fight.

··· *1951* ···

自从新中国第一个女拖拉机手——梁军出现后，许多年轻女性便渴望成为拖拉机手。农业部在双桥成立了机耕学校，有计划地吸收农村妇女参加学习。图为1951年3月，正在实习中的农业部京郊拖拉机站的第一批女拖拉机队队员合影

Liang Jun was the first female tractor driver of the PRC. To satisfy the need of many young women who were eager to be tractor drivers, the Ministry of Agriculture set up a mechanized farming school at Shuangqiao Farm in Beijing to provide them with systematic learning. The picture shows the first batch of female tractor drivers in the Beijing Suburb Tractor Station of the Ministry of Agriculture in March 1951.

## ··· *1951* ···

20 世纪 50 年代，毛泽东在全国体总成立大会上写下"发展体育运动，增强人民体质"的题词。这个时期，人民群众因地制宜，开展以广播操、跑步、乒乓球、羽毛球、游泳为主的体育活动。图为 1951 年 12 月，上海南洋模范中学的学生在做广播体操

In the 1950s, Mao Zedong wrote the inscription "Promote physical culture and sports; strengthening the people's physiques" at the founding of the All-China Sports Federation. During this period, the Chinese people adapted themselves to local conditions and carried out sports activities including radio gymnastics, running, table tennis, badminton and swimming. The picture shows students of Nanyang Model Middle School in Shanghai undergoing China's first set of radio gymnastics in December 1951.

### ··· *1952* ···

1952 年 2 月 10 日，河北省人民法院组织的公审大贪污犯刘青山、张子善大会在当时的省会保定举行。这是新中国第一起反腐大案

On February 10, 1952, the People's Court of Hebei Province organized a public trial of the corrupt officials, Liu Qingshan and Zhang Zishan, in Baoding, then capital of Hebei Province. This was the first major corruption case in the PRC.

**··· *1952* ···**

1952 年 6 月 13 日，新中国成立后修建的第一条铁路干线——成渝铁路竣工，7 月 1 日正式通车。图为 7 月 2 日，自重庆开出的第一列火车到达成都时受到群众的热烈欢迎

The Chengdu-Chongqing Railway, first trunk line built after the founding of the PRC, was completed on June 13, 1952, and opened to traffic on July 1. The picture shows the first train from Chongqing arriving in Chengdu on July 2 to a warm welcome from the people there.

**···1952···**

1952 年 11 月 15 日，中央人民政府扫除文盲工作委员会成立。新中国成立初期，我国的文盲率高达 80%，文盲成为新中国发展道路上的拦路虎。为解决这一问题，一场轰轰烈烈的扫盲运动在全国展开。图为山西省平顺具西沟村李顺达农林畜牧生产合作社的妇女识字小组在上课

On November 15, 1952, the Central People's Government Working Committee for the Elimination of Illiteracy was established. In the early days of the founding of the PRC, the illiteracy rate was as high as 80%. Illiteracy became a roadblock to the development of the new-born People's Republic. To solve this problem, a vigorous literacy campaign was launched throughout the country. The picture shows the women's literacy group of Li Shunda Agriculture, Forestry and Animal Husbandry Co-operative in Xigou Village, Pingshun County, Shanxi Province.

1953 年是我国第一个五年计划的开始，国家集中力量建设鞍钢。20 世纪 50 年代的鞍山钢铁公司，钢铁产量一度占据了全国的半壁江山。图为鞍钢机械总厂的革新能手王崇伦（右一）和工人们一起研究改进工具和生产的方法

China's First Five-Year Plan was launched in 1953, with efforts concentrated on construction of the Anshan Iron and Steel Works (AISW) in Liaoning Province. In the 1950s, the AISW's steel production once occupied half of national output. The picture shows Wang Chonglun (first right), a renovator of AISW General Machinery Plant, discussing new tools with his fellow workers.

··· **1953** ···

1953 年 10 月，新中国第一部彩色电影《梁山伯与祝英台》摄制完成。图为片中的主演粤剧名家袁雪芬和范瑞娟

In October 1953, the PRC's first color film *The Butterfly Lovers* was produced. The picture shows Yuan Xuefen and Fan Ruijuan, both famous Cantonese opera stars playing Liang Shanbo and Zhu Yintai, the film's chief roles.

### *1954*

1954 年 3 月 20 日，我国第一艘自行设计和制造的 5000 吨大客轮"民众号"从上海起航驶往重庆。图为轮船抵达雾都重庆时，群众举着鲜花迎接

On March 30, 1954, China's first self-designed and self-made 5,000-ton passenger ship, *People*, made its first voyage from Shanghai, arriving in fog-bound Chongqing, where the people celebrated with flowers.

## ··· *1954* ···

1954 年 4 月 26 日至 7 月 21 日，新中国首次以五大国之一的身份参加日内瓦会议，
讨论和平解决朝鲜问题和恢复印度支那和平问题。这是新中国首次登上国际舞台。图
为 1954 年日内瓦会议的最后一次全体会议

From April 26 to July 21, 1954, the PRC participated in the Geneva Conference for the first time as
one of the five major world powers to discuss the peaceful settlement of the Korean issue and the
restoration of peace in Indochina. This was the first appearance of the PRC on the international
stage. The picture shows the last plenary meeting of the 1954 Geneva Conference.

## … *1954* …

1954年9月，我国颁布了《中华人民共和国宪法》，这是新中国的第一部宪法。此前，1949年9月通过的《中国人民政治协商会议共同纲领》一直起着"临时宪法"的作用。图为1954年国庆节，游行群众抬着《中华人民共和国宪法》模型通过天安门

In September 1954, the PRC promulgated the Constitution of the People's Republic of China. This is the first constitution of the PRC. Prior to that, The Common Programme adopted in September 1949 had been playing the role of the Interim Constitution. The picture shows people in Beijing carried the model of the Constitution of the People's Republic of China through Tian'anmen Square on the National Day of 1954.

1955 年 4 月 18 日至 24 日，周恩来率中国代表团出席在印度尼西亚万隆举行的亚非会议。这是第一次由亚非国家发起的大型国际会议。会议形成了和平共处、求同存异的"万隆精神"。图为万隆亚非会议会场内景

From April 18 to 24, 1955, Zhou Enlai, then Premier of the State Council of the PRC, led the Chinese delegation to attend the Asia-Africa Conference in Bandung, Indonesia. That was the first large-scale international conference sponsored by Asian and African countries. It showed the Bandung Spirit featuring peaceful coexistence and seeking common ground while reserving differences. The picture shows the venue in Bandung.

··· **1955** ···

1955 年 7 月 6 日，克拉玛依一号井开钻，10 月 29 日完钻后喷出工业油流，宣告了新中国第一个大油田的诞生

On July 6, 1955, drilling of the Karamay No.1 Oil Well began. On October 29, industrial oil flowed out of the well, marking the birth of the first large oil field in the PRC.

## ·· *1956* ··

1955 年下半年至 1956 年年底，是我国农业合作化运动迅猛发展的时期。到 1956 年年底，我国基本上完成了社会主义改造，完成了由农民个体所有制到社会主义集体所有制的转变。图为 1956 年 1 月，群众在天安门广场游行，庆祝农业合作化运动胜利完

From the second half of 1955 to the end of 1956, China's agricultural cooperative movement developed rapidly. By the end of 1956, China had basically achieved complete socialist transformation and completed the transformation from individual ownership of peasants to collective ownership of socialism. The picture shows peasants parade in Tian'anmen Square to celebrate the successful completion of the agricultural cooperative movement in January 1956.

## ··· *1956* ···

1956 年 7 月 15 日，长春第一汽车制造厂生产出中国第一辆解放牌汽车。解放牌汽车的问世，结束了我国不能生产汽车的历史。图为第一批国产解放牌载重汽车排成长列开出长春第一汽车制造厂的时候，全厂职工夹道欢呼

On July 15, 1956, the Changchun No.1 Automobile Factory produced the PRC's first Jiefang brand motor vehicles. This has ended the history that China could not produce automobiles. The picture shows the first batch of Jiefang trucks queuing up to leave the Changchun Plant.

## ···*1956*···

1956 年年初，在全国范围内出现了社会主义改造高潮，资本主义工商业实现了全行业公私合营。图为 1956 年，上海市的永安公司实行公私合营，人们在门前庆祝

In early 1956, a nationwide climax of socialist transformation emerged and capitalist industry and commerce had realized public-private partnership in the whole industry. Here, the Yong'an Company in Shanghai began joint operation by public and private sectors. Employees celebrated in front of the company entrance.

1957 年 4 月 25 日，第一届中国出口商品交易会在广州举行（简称"广交会"）。以后每年在广州举办春秋季两次出口商品交易会，从 2007 年起改称中国进出口商品交易会。截至 2019 年 5 月，"广交会"已成功举办 125 届。图为第一届中国出口商品交易会上的工业样品陈列馆

On April 25, 1957, the first China Export Commodities Fair was held in Guangzhou, Guangdong Province. Since then, it has been held in the city twice a year, respectively in spring and autumn; it was renamed China Import and Export Commodities Fair from 2007. As of May 2019, the Fair has successfully been held 125 times. The picture shows the industrial exhibition hall at the first China Export Commodities Fair.

*··· 1957 ···*

1957 年 10 月 5 日，世界上海拔最高的公路——新藏公路建成通车。公路自新疆南部叶城至西藏阿里地区的拉孜县。图为从新疆开出的载重汽车通过海拔 4000 米高原上的大桥

On October 5, 1957, the Xinjiang-Tibet Highway, at the world's highest elevation, was opened to traffic. It runs from Yecheng County in Southern Xinjiang to Lhaze County in Ngari of Tibet. The picture shows trucks from Xinjiang driving across a bridge on the plateau at an altitude of 4,000 meters.

**1957**

1957 年 10 月 8 日，中国第一个天然石油基地——玉门油矿基本建成。图为两位工人在分析泥浆，了解玉门油矿新油井钻探情况

On October 8, 1957, the Yumen Oilfield, China's first natural oil base, was basically completed. The picture shows two workers analyzing mud to understand the drilling situation of a new well in the Yumen Oilfield.

*…1957…*

1957 年 10 月 15 日，新中国第一座跨越长江的公路、铁路两用大桥——武汉长江大桥举行通车典礼，从此南北天堑变通途

On October 15, 1957, the Wuhan Yangtze River Bridge, the first highway-railway bridge spanning the Yangtze River, was opened to traffic. This was a huge benefit for North-South transportation.

## ···1958···

20 世纪 50 年代，收音机可以算是高档家电，能拥有一台收音机是当时家庭生活富裕的标志。图为 1958 年 4 月，北京某大杂院的孩子们围在收音机旁收听中央人民广播电台的少年儿童广播节目

In the 1950s, radios were regarded as high-end household appliances. Having a radio was the benchmark of the prosperity of family life at that time. In April 1958, children from a large complex in Beijing gather around the radio to listen to a program from the Central People's Broadcasting Station.

### ··· *1958* ···

1958 年 9 月 2 日，新中国第一座国家电视台——北京电视台（中央电视台前身），开始对首都地区正式播出黑白电视节目。1978 年 5 月 1 日起更名为中央电视台。图为主持人在演播室录制节目

On September 2, 1958, Beijing Television, the first national television station in the PRC, began broadcasting in black-and-white in the Beijing area. On May 1, 1978, it was renamed CCTV. The picture shows the hosts recording a program in the studio.

## ··· *1959* ···

← 1959 年，在联邦德国举行的第二十五届世乒赛上，容国团为中国队夺得世界男子单打冠军，成为新中国第一个世界冠军。图为 4 月 22 日容国团载誉归来

In 1959, at the 25th World Table Tennis Championships held in Dortmund of the then West Germany, the Chinese men's player Rong Guotuan won the singles title to become the first world champion of the PRC. The picture shows Rong Guotuan returning to Beijing on April 22, 1959.

→ 1959 年 9 月 13 日至 10 月 3 日，第一届"全运会"在北京举行，这是中国首次举办全国性大型运动会，截至 2019 年，"全运会"已成功举办 13 届。图为 1959 年 9 月 13 日，运动员在开幕式上列队步入会场

The PRC held its first National Games in Beijing from September 13 to October 3 in 1959, the first time the PRC held a large-scale ports event. As of 2019, the PRC has successfully held 13 National Games. The picture shows the opening ceremony on September 13, 1959.

**···1959···**

1959 年 9 月 26 日，中国石油勘探队在东北松辽盆地陆相沉积中找到了工业性油流。时值国庆 10 周年，因此将油田命名为"大庆"。大庆油田的发现，打破了地质学界长期存在的"中国贫油论"。图为 1959 年，黑龙江大庆油田第一口油井试喷成功，工人欢呼庆祝

On September 26, 1959, the China Petroleum Exploration Team found industrial oil flow in the continental deposits of the Songliao Basin in Northeast China. As it took place at the time of the 10th anniversary of the founding of the PRC, the oilfield was named "Daqing" meaning "great celebration". The discovery of the Daqing Oilfield broke the long-standing theory of China being poor in oil resources in the field of geology. The picture shows the first successful oil well blowout test in 1959.

## ··· 1960 ···

20 世纪 60 年代，那个时代物质没有现在这么丰富，但是过年的氛围却非常浓郁。过年的时候人们都会贴春联，有文化的人还会帮助大家写春联。图为 1960 年春节，辽宁省沈阳市郊五三人民公社社员刘乃庚一家在写春联、贴年画，喜迎春节

In the 1960s, the material was not as rich as it is now, but the atmosphere of the Spring Festival or the lunar New Year was very strong. Spring Festival couplets were put up for the festival. The picture shows Liu Naigeng and his family members from the Wusan People's Commune in Shenyang, Liaoning Province, writing couplets and pasting lunar New Year pictures to celebrate the occasion in 1960.

### *1960*

1960 年 5 月 25 日清晨 4 点 20 分，中国登山队队员王富洲、贡布（藏族）、屈银华胜利登上了海拔 8848 米的珠穆朗玛峰。这是人类历史上第一次从北坡登上世界第一高峰。图为我国登山队队员在海拔 7150 米的冰雪坡上行军

At 4:20 a.m. on May 25, 1960, Chinese mountaineers Wang Fuzhou, Kungbo (Tibetan) and Qu Yinhua successfully reached the top of Mount Qomolangma at an altitude of 8,848 meters. This is the first successful climb from the northern side of the world's highest peak. The picture shows the climbing party at a height of 7,150 meters.

## ···· 1961 ····

20 世纪 60 年代，对于孩子们来说，春节永远是快乐的。平日里没有零花钱，春节里糊个纸灯笼，红色小鞭炮拆开来单个儿放，都能让快乐延续一年。图为 1961 年春节，在江苏省南京市夫子庙花灯市场上，人们在选购花灯

In the 1960s, the Spring Festival was always happy for children. Paper lanterns were made for fun, and red firecrackers were lit one by one. Such happiness would last for one year in mind. Here is a shot of the lanterns market at the Confucius Temple in Nanjing, Jiangsu Province during the Spring Festival in February 1961.

··· *1961* ···

1961 年 9 月 21 日，山西省闻喜县东镇供销合作社的工作人员
在包装月饼，准备供应中秋节市场。那时候的月饼做工都非常
简单，大多为果仁馅，是当时中秋节非常珍贵的节日食物

On September 21, 1961, the staff of the Dongzhen Supply and Marketing
Cooperative in Wenxi County, Shanxi Province, were packing moon cakes
to prepare for the Mid-Autumn Festival celebrations by local farmers. At
that time, the moon cakes were very simple, mostly filled with nuts. They
were very precious food for the Mid-Autumn Festival.

**··· 1962 ···**

1962年5月22日，第一届电影"百花奖"颁奖典礼在北京举行。"百花奖"是由《大众电影》杂志社主办的一年一度的群众性评奖，和"金鸡奖"一起并称为中国电影双奖。图为时任中国文联主席的郭沫若在典礼上为《红色娘子军》女演员祝希娟颁奖

On May 22, 1962, the first awards ceremony of the Hundred Flowers Award was held in Beijing. The Award was an annual mass appraisal award sponsored by *Popular Film* magazine, and form a double peak of achievement with the Golden Rooster Award in the Chinese film industry. The picture shows Guo Moruo (1892-1978), then President of the Chinese Federation of Literature, presenting an award to Zhu Xijuan (right), the actress of *Red Detachment of Women*.

混纺

··· **1962** ···

涤棉混纺织物是我国在 20 世纪 60 年代初期开发的一个纺织品种，深受广大消费者的喜爱。图为 1962 年 9 月 22 日，在上海南京路的南洋袜衫商店里，顾客们正在选购用合成纤维和棉花混纺织成的棉毛衫

Polyester-cotton blended fabric, a kind of textile developed in the early 1960s in China, was very popular with Chinese consumers. The picture shows that customers buying cotton sweaters made of synthetic fibers and cotton at the Nanyang Socks Shop on Nanjing Road, Shanghai, on September 22, 1962.

## 1963

1963 年 1 月，上海第六人民医院外科医师陈中伟将青年工人王存柏被机器完全轧断的右手成功地重新接合了起来。这是中国第一例成功的前臂完全性创伤断肢再植手术。图为陈中伟主治医生（右）等在观察王存柏的手腕恢复情况

In January 1963, Dr. Chen Zhongwei of Shanghai No.6 People's Hospital successfully reconnected the right hand of young worker Wang Cunbai that had been completely severed by a machine. This was the first successful forearm amputation and limb restoration operation in China. The picture shows Dr. Chen Zhongwei (right) and others observing Wang Cunbai's wrist recovery action.

··· *1963* ···

20 世纪 60 年代，北方百姓的冬季活动多为冰上运动。当时在北京流行一句话："在冰上摔倒劈叉，是对冬天基本的尊重。" 1963 年冬天，在北京什刹海体育场和北海体育场举办了一次"体育庙会"。图为滑冰爱好者在"体育庙会"的冰场上表演"大头娃娃"

In the 1960s, the winter activities of the northern people were mostly ice sports. There was a popular saying in Beijing at that time: "Falling on the ice is a basic respect for winter." In the winter of 1963, a "sports temple fair" was held at the Beijing Shichahai Stadium and the Beihai Stadium. The picture shows skaters performing "Big Head Doll" on the ice rink.

# ··· *1963* ···

1963 年 3 月 5 日，《人民日报》发表毛泽东"向雷锋同志学习"的题词。全国掀起学习雷锋先进事迹的热潮。自此之后，每年 3 月成为"学雷锋活动月"。图为 3 月 19 日，"雷锋同志模范事迹展览"在中国人民革命军事博物馆开幕

On March 5, 1963, *People's Daily* published Mao Zedong's inscription "Learning from Comrade Lei Feng". This touched off a wave of "learning from Lei Feng" and March became the "Learning from Leifeng Month" every year. The picture shows the opening of the Lei Feng Exhibition at the People's Revolutionary Military Museum of China on March 19, 1963.

··· *1964* ···

1964 年 2 月 5 日，中共中央发出《关于传达石油工业部关于大庆石油会战情况的报告的通知》。"工业学大庆"运动在全国展开。图为以艰苦奋斗而闻名的"铁人"——钻井第二大队大队长王进喜（左二），正在参加钻井劳动

On February 5, 1964, the CPC Central Committee issued the Notice on the Report of the Ministry of Petroleum Industry on the Daqing Oilfield Battle. From then on, a campaign was launched to learn from Daqing in industry. The picture shows Wang Jinxi (second left), captain of the Second Drilling Brigade, who is known for his hard work, taking part in drilling work.

1964 年 2 月 10 日，《人民日报》发表社论和通讯，介绍山西省昔阳县大寨大队艰苦奋斗、发展生产的事迹。此后，"农业学大寨"运动在全国展开。图为大寨大队的带头人——大寨大队党支部的成员带领社员下地劳动

On February 10, 1964, *People's Daily* published an editorial and a newsletter introducing the hard struggle made by the Dazhai Production Brigade in Xiyang County, Shanxi Province. Since then, the "Learning from Dazhai in agriculture" campaign spread throughout the country. The picture shows members of the Party Branch of the Dazhai Production Brigade working together with the commune members in the field.

# ··· *1964* ···

1964 年 10 月，正值中华人民共和国
成立 15 周年，3000 多名专业和业余
文艺工作者，为世界各国贵宾表演大
型音乐舞蹈史诗《东方红》

In October 1964, on the 15th anniversary
of the founding of the PRC, more than
3,000 professional and amateur literary and
artistic workers performed the large-scale
musical and dance epic *The East is Red* for
distinguished guests who came to Beijing to
attend the celebration of National Day.

## ··· 1964 ···

1964 年 10 月 16 日，中国第一颗原子弹爆炸成功，标志着国防建设进入了一个新阶段。图为人民群众游行庆祝原子弹爆炸成功

On October 16, 1964, the PRC successfully exploded its first atomic bomb, marking a new stage of national defense construction. The picture shows people marching to celebrate.

## ···1965···

1965 年 9 月 17 日，我国科学工作者经过 6 年 9 个月的艰苦工作，在世界上第一次用人工的方法合成了一种具有生物活力的蛋白质——结晶胰岛素。图为科研人员将人工合成的蛋白质注入小白鼠体内，测验它的生物活力

On September 17, 1965, after six years and nine months of hard work, Chinese scientists synthesized a bioactive protein - crystalline insulin - for the first time in the world. The picture shows the team of Chinese scientists inject synthetic products into mice to test their biological activity.

20 世纪五六十年代，全国各地响应毛主席"知识青年到农村去，接受贫下中农的再教育"的号召，组织大量城市"知识青年"离开城市，在农村定居和劳动。图为1965 年，吉林省城市应届毕业生到农村参加劳动

In the 1950s and 1960s, a large number of urban "educated youths" answered Chairman Mao Zedong's call to "receive re-education from the poor and lower middle peasants" and were organized throughout the country to settle down and work in the countryside. In 1965, the high school graduates in Jilin Province went to work in the countryside.

**⋯ *1966* ⋯**

1966 年 1 月，我国自行设计和建造的第一艘综合性海洋科学考察船"东方红号"
在海上进行考察活动

In January 1966, *Dongfanghong*, the first comprehensive marine scientific research vessel designed and built by China, underwent sea trials.

## ··· *1966* ···

红旗渠是从太行山山腰修建的引漳入林的工程，被称为"人工天河"。1966年4月20日，红旗渠三条干渠全部竣工通水。图为在红旗渠修建过程中，工人们在峭壁上开凿水渠

The Red Flag Canal is a project built from the mountainside of Taihang Mountains to introduce Zhanghe River water into the forest area. On April 20, 1966, all three main canals of the Red Flag Canal were opened to water. The picture shows workers digging on the cliff.

## ··· *1967* ···

1967 年 6 月 17 日上午，我国第一颗氢弹爆炸试验成功。从第一颗原子弹爆炸到第一颗氢弹爆炸试验成功，中国用了 2 年 8 个月，研制成功的速度是世界上最快的。图为氢弹爆炸现场

On the morning of June 17, 1967, China's first successful hydrogen bomb test took place. It took two years and eight months for China to explode successfully the first atomic bomb and the first hydrogen bomb. The speed of successful development is the fastest in the world. The picture is taken during the evacuation after taking shots of the mushroom cloud downwind.

## ··· *1968* ···

1968 年 10 月，上海京剧院演出的革命现代京剧《智取威虎山》。该剧是当时革命样板戏代表性作品之一

In October 1968, the revolutionary modern Peking Opera *The Taking of Tiger Mountain* was performed by the Shanghai Peking Opera House. This was one of representative revolutionary model dramas being performed at that time.

··· *1968* ···

1968 年 12 月 29 日，南京长江大桥
全面建成通车，它是长江上第一座由
我国自行设计和建造的双层式铁路、
公路两用桥梁，在中国桥梁史和世界
桥梁史上具有重要意义，是中国经济
建设的重要成就、中国桥梁建设的重
要里程碑。图为南京长江大桥公路桥
举行通车典礼

On December 29, 1968, the Nanjing Yangtze
River Bridge, the first double-deck railway
and highway bridge designed and built by
China itself, was opened to traffic. It is of
great significance in the history of bridges
in China and in the history of bridges in the
world. It is also an important achievement
in China's economic construction and
an important milestone in China's bridge
construction. The picture shows the opening
ceremony of the highway bridge.

## ··· *1969* ···

1969 年，中国医疗队的医务人员在阿尔及利亚的撒哈拉沙漠牧区为牧民看病。自 1963 年向非洲派出第一支医疗队之后的 6 年间，中国已向 47 个非洲国家和地区派出了 1.6 万名医务工作者，救助非洲民众 2.4 亿人次

A shot of the Chinese medical team in Algeria visiting herdsmen in the Sahara Desert pastoral area in 1969. In the six years since the first medical team was dispatched to Africa in 1963, the PRC sent 16,000 medical workers to 47 African countries, providing medical aids to 240 million people.

## *1969*

1969 年 10 月 1 日，新中国第一条地下铁道线路在北京建成，并在 1971 年宣布试运营。后于 1981 年正式对外开放，成为了世界上最繁忙的地铁线路。图为 1981 年前门地铁站

On October 1, 1969, the first subway line in the PRC was completed in Beijing, and its trial operation was announced two years later. It was officially opened to full traffic in 1981 and became the busiest subway line in the world. The picture shows the Qianmen Metro Station in 1981.

热烈欢呼我国第一颗人
造地球卫星发射成功！

## ··· 1970 ···

1970 年 4 月 24 日，中国在第一个火
箭发射试验基地——酒泉卫星发射中
心成功发射第一颗人造地球卫星"东
方红一号"，成为世界上第五个独立
研制和发射卫星的国家。图为电话接
线员们在看报纸，为中国第一颗人造
地球卫星发射成功欢喜不已

On April 24, 1970, the PRC successfully
launched its first artificial earth satellite,
*Dongfanghong-1*, from the Jiuquan Satellite
Launch Center, its first rocket launch
experimental base. China became the fifth
country in the world to independently
develop and launch satellites. The picture
shows communications staff rejoicing at the
successful launch.

### ··· *1970* ···

1970 年 12 月 26 日，我国第一艘核
潜艇下水。1971 年 8 月 22 日，我国
第一艘核潜艇首次以核动力驶向试验
海区，进行航行试验。1974 年 8 月 1
日，我国第一艘核潜艇正式编入海军
战斗序列

On December 26, 1970, the PRC launched
its first nuclear submarine. On August 22,
1971, the vessel underwent sea trials under
nuclear power for the first time. It joined the
naval combat fleet on August 1, 1974.

### ··· *1971* ···

1971 年 4 月 10 日，美国乒乓球代表团应邀访华，被称为"小球转动了大球"的"乒乓外交"由此开启。图为美国乒乓球运动员格伦·科恩被好奇的中国人团团围住

On April 10, 1971, a US table tennis delegation was invited to visit China, launching "Ping Pong diplomacy" known as "a small ball turning a big ball". The picture shows Glenn Cowan, an American table tennis player, surrounded by curious Chinese.

··· *1971* ···

1971 年 10 月，第二十六届联合国大会以压倒多数通过了关于恢复中华人民共和国在联合国的
一切合法权利的决议。在此后的几十年里，中国国际地位日益提高。今天，在联合国的几乎所
有机构里都可以看到中国代表的身影，他们以充满活力的姿态发挥着中国作为常任理事国之一
的作用。图为第二十六届联合国大会会议现场

In October 1971, the 26th UN General Assembly adopted by an overwhelming majority a resolution on
the restoration of all legitimate rights of the PRC in the United Nations. In the following decades, China's
international status has been rising. Today, the representatives of the PRC can be seen in almost all the organs of
the United Nations and China plays a dynamic role as one of the permanent members of the United Nations.
The picture shows the scene of the General Assembly.

## ··· *1972* ···

1972 年 2 月 21 日，美国总统尼克松
到达北京。这是美国总统第一次访问
中华人民共和国。2 月 28 日，两国在
上海发表《联合公报》，标志着两国
关系正常化进程的开始。从此，中美
两国关系进入了一个新的历史时期。
图为 2 月 25 日，尼克松夫妇在北京故
宫参观

On February 21, 1972, Richard Milhous
Nixon (1913-1994), 37th President of the
United States, arrived in Beijing. This was the
first time that the President of the United
States visited the PRC. On February 28,
the two countries issued the Shanghai Joint
Communique announcing the normalization
of Sino-US relations. Since then, the
relationship between China and the United
States has entered a new historical period.
The picture shows President Nixon and his
wife visiting the Beijing Palace Museum on
February 25.

··· *1972* ···

20世纪70年代，湛江已经成为我国南海的重要水产基地。在那个年代，由于全国农产品和畜牧、水产品产量逐渐增加，城乡粮食和副食品供应也逐渐丰富。图为1972年2月，一家海味店出售鱿鱼、虾米、鱼翅等各种海味

In the 1970s, Zhanjiang in Guangdong Province became an important fishery base in the South China Sea. During that period, as the output of agricultural products, animal husbandry and aquatic products increased gradually, the supply of grain and non-staple food in urban and rural areas was also gradually enriched. The picture shows a seafood store selling squid, shrimp, shark's fin and other seafood in February 1972.

**··· 1973 ···**

1973 年 8 月 26 日，中国第一台每秒运算 100 万次的集成电路电子计算机研制成功。图为工作人员在启动计算机算题

On August 26, 1973, China's first integrated circuit computer with one million operations per second was successfully designed and developed. The picture shows workers engage in problem solving.

**1973**

1973年10月，在全国水稻科研会议上，袁隆平发表了《利用"野稗"选育"三系"的进展》一文，正式宣告中国籼型杂交水稻"三系"配套成功。自此，袁隆平率领科研团队，在数年时间内解决了十多亿人的吃饭问题。图为袁隆平（右三）在观察杂交水稻生长情况

On October 1973, at the National Conference on Rice Science and Technology, Yuan Longping published his *Report on Development of Three Lines in Hybrid Rice through Wild Abortive Rice*, officially confirming the success of production of Indica Hybrid Rice in China. Since then, Yuan Longping and his scientific research team have solved the food problem for more than a billion people in a few years. The picture shows Yuan Longping (third right) observing the growth of the hybrid rice.

## ··· *1974* ···

1974 年 9 月 1 日至 16 日，中国体育代表团参加了在伊朗首都德黑兰举行的第七届亚运会。这是新中国成立以来首次参加亚运会，并参加其中 14 个项目的比赛。图为中国体育代表团在第七届亚运会开幕式上入场

From September 1 to 16, 1974, the Chinese sports delegation participated in the 7th Asian Games held in Tehran, capital of the Islamic Republic of Iran. This was the first time that the PRC participated in the Asian Games, providing competitors in 14 events. The picture shows the entry of the Chinese sports delegation at the opening ceremony.

# ···*1974*···

1974 年 9 月 15 日，黄河青铜峡水利
枢纽工程基本建成。青铜峡水利枢纽
工程于 1958 年 8 月动工兴建，是黄
河梯级第一期开发的大型水利工程之
一。枢纽的兴建结束了宁夏灌区两千
多年无坝引水的历史。图为正在建设
中的青铜峡水利枢纽

On September 15, 1974, the Qingtongxia
Water Conservancy Project on the Yellow
River was basically completed. Construction
began in August 1958 as one of the large-
scale water conservancy projects developed
in the first stage of the Yellow River cascade.
The construction of the hub has ended the
history of more than 2,000 years of dam-
free water diversion in the Ningxia irrigation
areas. The picture shows the Qingtongxia
Water Conservancy Project under
construction.

··· *1974* ···

1974 年 9 月 28 日，中国第二大油田——胜利油田建成。胜利油田在华北这片被认为"不可能有油"的地方建成，其成就和经验，丰富和发展了我国油田勘探、开发的理论，对加速我国同类地区油田的勘探、开发工作有很大意义。图为胜利油田一口油井正在试油

On September 28, 1974, the Shengli Oilfield, the second largest oilfield in the PRC, was completed. The Shengli Oilfield was built in North China, which is considered "impossible to have oil". Its achievements enrich and develop the theory of oil field exploration and development in China, and have great significance in accelerating the exploration and development of oilfields in similar areas in China.The picture shows an oil well in the Shengli Oilfield being tested.

## ···*1975*···

1975年2月4日，中国当时最大的水电站——刘家峡水电站建成。水电站位于甘肃省永靖县境内，以黄河水为动力，总发电能力为122.5万千瓦，一年能发电57亿度。图为刘家峡水电站施工工地正在吊运水涡轮

On February 4, 1975, the Liujiaxia Hydropower Station, the largest hydropower station in the PRC at that time, was completed. Located in Yongjing County, Gansu Province, the power station is powered by the water of the Yellow River, with a total power generation capacity of 1.225 million kilowatts and annual power generation capacity of 5.7 billion kWh of electricity. The picture shows the water turbine being hoisted at the construction site of the Liujiaxia Hydropower Station.

## ··· *1975* ···

1975 年 7 月 1 日，中国第一条电气化铁路——宝成铁路建成通车。宝成铁路全长676 公里。图为中国自制的"韶山"型电力机车牵引着客车行驶在宝成铁路上

On July 1, 1975, China's first electrified railway, the Baoji (Shaanxi Province)-Chengdu (Sichuan Province) Railway, was completed and opened to traffic. This railway is 676 km long. The picture shows the self-made *Shaoshan* electric locomotive pulling a line of passenger carriages on the line.

## ··· *1975* ···

1975 年 11 月 26 日，我国第一颗返回式遥感卫星在酒泉卫星发射中心顺利发射升空，后按预定计划安全返回祖国大地，使中国成为了世界上第三个掌握卫星回收技术的国家。图为"长征二号"运载火箭托举我国第一颗返回式遥感卫星从酒泉卫星发射中心发射升空

On November 26, 1975, the PRC's first recoverable remote sensing satellite was launched successfully at the Jiuquan Satellite Launch Center, and then recovered safely as scheduled, making the PRC the third country in the world to master the technology. The picture shows the launch from the Jiuquan Satellite Launch Center using a Long March 2 rocket.

**····1975····**

在 20 世纪 70 年代，文化生活十分匮乏。各个工厂为加强文化宣传，丰富职工的业余生活，都会组建阵容强大的文艺宣传队。工厂还会经常举办文艺演出，邀请专业团体或其他工厂文艺宣传队来厂演出。图为 1975 年 12 月，上海乐团在北京第三通用机械厂为工人演出

In the 1970s, cultural life was scarce in China. In order to strengthen cultural publicity and enrich the spare-time life of workers and staff, most factories formed their own literary and artistic publicity teams. The factories often organized professional groups or groups from other factories to perform in the factory. The picture shows the Shanghai Orchestra performing for workers at the Beijing Third General Machinery Factory in December 1975.

··· *1976* ···

1976 年 1 月 8 日，周恩来在北京逝世，享年 78 岁。图为人们抬着周总理画像走向人民英雄纪念碑

On January 8, 1976, Zhou Enlai passed away in Beijing at the age of 78. The picture shows people carrying the portrait of Premier Zhou to the Monument to the People's Heroes at Tian'anmen Square in Beijing.

··· **1976** ···

1976 年 9 月 9 日，毛泽东在北京逝
世，享年 83 岁。图为 9 月 18 日，首
都百万群众在天安门广场隆重举行追
悼大会

On September 9, 1976, Mao Zedong passed
away in Beijing at the age of 83. The picture
shows commemorations on September 18 at
Tian'anmen Square.

1976 年 10 月 21 日，首都 150 万群众举行盛大游行，热烈庆祝粉碎"四人帮"的伟大胜利

On October 21, 1976, some 1.5 million people in Beijing held a grand parade to celebrate the smashing of the "Gang of Four", which marked the end of the chaotic "cultural revolution" (1966-1976).

## 1977

20 世纪 70 年代，由于物资紧张，城市居民使用副食本购买油、盐、肉、蛋、麻酱等许多副食品。到了 70 年代末期，市场上的副食品种类和数量明显增多。图为 1977 年 2 月，广西壮族自治区食品工业部门生产多种糖果，供应市场需要

In the 1970s, due to the shortage of materials, urban residents were issued non-staple food books for the purchase of many non-staple foods such as edible oil, salt, meat, eggs, sesame paste and so on. By the end of the 1970s, the varies and quantities of non-staple foods on the market had increased significantly. The picture shows that in February 1977, the food industry of Guangxi Zhuang Autonomous Region produced a variety of candies to meet growing market needs. Here is a candy store in Nanning, capital of Guangxi.

### ··· *1977* ···

1977 年 5 月，在广西隆林各族自治县德峨公社安家落户的医务人员，制作了适合马驮的药箱，装上常用药品和医疗器械，巡回在壮乡苗寨，为山区人民的健康服务

On May 1977, medical workers who settled down in the De'e People's Commune, Longlin Ethnic Autonomous County, Guangxi Zhuang Autonomous Region, pack boxes of commonly-used medicines and medical devices, suitable for horses to carry on their backs during a medical treatment program for Miao ethnic villagers.

··· *1977* ···

1977 年 9 月，教育部在北京召开全国
高等学校招生工作会议，决定恢复已
经停止了 10 年的全国高等院校招生
考试。图为 1977 年，清华大学恢复
高考后的第一批大学生在课堂上学习

In September 1977, the Ministry of
Education convened a national conference
on college enrollment in Beijing, and
decided to resume the national college
entrance examination suspended for 10
years. The picture shows the first batch
of undergraduates in class after Tsinghua
University in Beijing resumed the practice
in 1977.

# 第二章 富起来

## Chapter II Chinese People Are Getting Rich

1978 年 12 月召开的中共十一届三中全会，实现了中华人民共和国成立以来党的历史上具有深远意义的伟大转折，开启了改革开放和社会主义现代化建设的新时期。

改革开放以来，中国共产党把马克思主义基本原理同中国实际和时代特点相结合，不断推进理论创新、实践创新、制度创新、文化创新以及各方面创新，成功开创、坚持和发展了中国特色社会主义。改革开放极大地激发了人民群众的积极性、主动性、创造性，极大地解放和发展了社会生产力，极大地增强社会发展活力。人民生活显著改善，综合国力显著增强，国际地位显著提高。

百姓的衣着从"黑灰"走向"个性"；饮食从"解决温饱"走向"吃出健康"；住房从"蜗居"走向"广厦"；出行方式从"单一"走向"多元"；生活用品从"三大件"到如今层出不穷的高科技产品；教育发展日新月异，教育系统日臻完善，国民受教育程度大大提高；科技发展势头迅猛，多个领域赶超世界先进水平……

在三十多年里，我国 GDP 年均增长近 10%，重要工农业产品的产量跃居世界前列。改革开放新时期，我国总体上解决了困扰几千年的忍饥挨饿、缺吃少穿、生活困顿的问题，迎来了从温饱不足到小康富裕的伟大飞跃！

The Third Plenary Session of the 11th CPC Central Committee, held in late December 1978, realized a great turning point of far-reaching significance in the history of the CPC since the founding of the PRC, and launched a new era of reform and opening up and socialist modernization construction.

Since the initiation of the reform and opening up program in late 1978, the CPC has combined the basic principles of Marxism with the reality of China and the characteristics of the times, constantly promoted theoretical, practical, institutional, cultural and other innovation, and successfully created, adhered to and developed socialism with Chinese characteristics. The reform and opening up program has greatly stimulated the enthusiasm, creativity and initiative of the people, and greatly emancipated and developed social productive forces, thereby greatly enhancing the vitality of social development. China has significantly improved living standards, overall national strength and greatly enhanced its international status.

In the same period, people's clothing changed from the prevailing "black/blue or/grey" to bright colors and stylish appearance; their diet changed from "having enough basic food and clothing" to "eating a healthy diet"; their housing changed from "humble dwelling" to being "spacious and well-decorated"; their travel mode changed from "single" to "pluralistic" ways; their daily necessities changed from "three major items [wrist, watch, bicycle and sewing machine]" to today's high-tech products; the education system is improving with each passing day, with the national education level greatly enhanced. Meanwhile, China experienced fast development in science and technology, with many fields having developed from a stage of catching up [with the West], through surpassing the world's advanced level to leading the global development trend.

In the past 30-odd years, China's GDP has increased by nearly 10% annually, and its output of major industrial and agricultural products is now in the forefront of the world. In the new period of reform and opening-up, China has solved the problems of hunger and starvation, lack of food and clothing, and hardship of life, which plagued the nation for thousands of years. It has ushered in a great leap from former insufficiency to well-off prosperity.

**1978**

1978 年 3 月 18 日至 31 日，全国科学大会在北京隆重举行。在大会上，邓小平同志提出的"科学技术是生产力"的著名论断，对国家长远发展具有十分重要的意义。图为 3 月 18 日，来自全国各地的科技界代表步入人民大会堂，参加全国科学大会

From March 18 to 31, 1978, the National Science Congress was held in a solemn atmosphere in Beijing. At the conference, Deng Xiaoping put forward his famous conclusion that science and technology were productive forces. This proved of great significance to the long-term development of the country. The picture shows representatives of the scientific and technological community from all over the country entering the Great Hall of the People in Beijing to attend the National Science Congress on March 18.

···*1978*···

1978 年 11 月 27 日，中国第一个自行设计、制造设备、施工安装的大型钢铁联合企业——攀枝花钢铁工业基地第一期工程正式建成投产。图为攀枝花钢铁公司生产的产品准备启运

On November 27, 1978, the Panzhihua Iron and Steel Industrial Base, China's first large-scale iron and steel complex to design, manufacture and install its own equipment, was formally completed and began operation. The picture shows products manufactured by Panzhihua Iron and Steel Company.

··· *1978* ···

1978 年 12 月，安徽省凤阳县梨园公社小岗生产队的 18 个农民在一份合同书上按下手印，"联产承包责任制"在全国拉开了序幕。小岗村因此被称为中国农村改革第一村。图为当年 18 个农民中的 3 位

In December 1978, a group of 18 farmers of the Xiaogang Production Team of Liyuan People's Commune in Fengyang County, Anhui Province, affix their handprints to a contract introducing the contract responsibility system for joint production, first of its kind in China. Xiaogang Village is therefore referred to as the pioneer of China's rural reform. The picture shows three of the 18 farmers.

··· *1978* ···

1978 年 12 月，中共十一届三中全会在北京召开。会议全面纠正了"文化大革命"的错误，重新确立党的马克思主义的思想路线、政治路线、组织路线，拨乱反正，解决了党的历史上一批重大冤假错案。会议决定把党和国家的工作重心转移到社会主义现代化建设上来。图为 12 月 24 日，北京市通县张家湾公社的干部和社员认真学习党的十一届三中全会公报

In December 1978, the Third Plenary Session of the 11th CPC Central Committee was held in Beijing. The conference corrected the mistakes of the "cultural revolution" in an all-round way, re-established the Party's Marxist ideological, political and organizational lines, took steps to rectify the chaos and solve a number of major injustices and false cases that had emerged in the Party's recent history. The meeting decided to shift the focus of Party and State work to the modernization drive. The picture shows members of the Zhangjiawan People's Commune in Tongxian County of Beijing earnestly studying the communique of the Third Plenary Session of the 11th CPC Central Committee.

## ··· *1979* ···

1979 年 1 月 1 日，中美两国正式建立外交关系，由此揭开了两国关系的新篇章，对国际形势和世界格局产生了重大而深远的影响。图为 1978 年 12 月 16 日，北京市民争阅《人民日报》关于中美即将建交的"号外"

On January 1, 1979, China and the United States formally established diplomatic relations, opening a new chapter in bilateral relations with significant and far-reaching impact on the international situation and the world pattern. The picture shows Beijing citizens scrambling to read the extra edition of the *People's Daily* about the forthcoming establishment of diplomatic relations between China and the United States.

## ··· *1979* ···

20 世纪 70 年代末期，中国百姓的衣橱开始出现颜色鲜艳的服装。在这之前，中国百姓的衣服基本上只有灰、蓝、黑三种颜色。图为 1979 年 8 月，成群结队的顾客在上海一家百货商店中挑选布料来制作色彩鲜艳的衣服

In the late 1970s, bright-colored clothes began to appear in China. Before that, clothing had been basically gray, blue and black. Picture shows shoppers gathering at a department store in Shanghai to choose cloth to make brightly colored clothes in August 1979.

## ··· *1979* ···

在 20 世纪 70 年代，自行车、缝纫机、手表被称为"三大件"。图为 1979 年，四川邛崃，前进公社社员在选购自行车

In the 1970s, in Qionglai, Sichuan Province, members of the Qianjin People's Commune buy bicycles that, together with sewing machines and watches, were called the "three big items" of consumer spending at that time.

## ··· *1980* ···

1980 年 4 月 10 日，北京航空食品公司被批准成立，5 月 1 日公司在北京正式挂牌。这是改革开放后内地第一家合资企业。图为北京航空食品公司厨师长、法国人孟培沙（左二）和助理厨师长邓耀全（右二）等在一起研究航空菜肴的配制

On April 10, 1980, the Beijing Air Catering Co., Ltd. was established. On May 1, the company was officially listed in Beijing, becoming the first Sino-foreign joint venture on the Chinese mainland after the introduction of the reform and opening up program begun in late 1978. The picture shows French chef Montessa (second left) of the Beijing Air Catering Co., Ltd. and assistant chef Deng Yaoquan (second right) studying the preparation of in-flight dishes together.

## ··· *1980* ···

1980 年 8 月 2 日至 7 日，中共中央召开全国劳动就业工作会议，提出实行"在国家统筹规划和指导下，劳动部门介绍就业、自愿组织起来就业和自谋职业相结合"的方针。图为 1980 年，内地第一家个体饭馆——悦宾饭馆在北京开业

From August 2 to 7, 1980, the CPC Central Committee held a national conference on employment, and put forward the policy that "under overall state planning and guidance, the labor department oversees employment opportunities, organizes employment voluntarily in combination with self-employment". The picture shows the Yuebin Restaurant, China's first privately owned restaurant established in Beijing in 1980.

## *1980*

1980 年 8 月，中国政府正式批准建立深圳、珠海、汕头、厦门经济特区，1988 年批准建立海南岛经济特区。图为可停泊 5000 吨货船的广东深圳经济特区蛇口工业区顺岸式码头

In August 1980, the Chinese government officially approved the establishment of the Shenzhen Special Economic Zone in Guangdong Province, followed by the establishment of special economic zones in Zhuhai and Shantou in the same province, and Xiamen in neighboring Fujian Province. In 1988, the Chinese government approved the Hainan Island Economic Zone in Hainan Province. The picture shows the parallel wharf of the Shekou Industrial Zone of the Shenzhen Special Economic Zone, able to berth 5,000-ton cargo ships.

## ··· *1980* ···

在 20 世纪七八十年代，交通警察的形象总是与圆柱形的红黄色交通岗楼联系在一起。在没有摄像头、自动交通信号灯的年代，岗楼是当时用于控制信号灯的场所。图为 1980 年，上海南京路，一名交警正在控制塔台上控制交通信号灯

In the 1970s and 1980s, the image of traffic policemen was always associated with the cylindrical red and yellow traffic guard structures. In the absence of cameras and automatic traffic lights, the traffic guard structures controlling signal lights at that time. The picture shows a traffic policeman controlling the lights on a control tower on Nanjing Road, Shanghai, in 1980.

··· *1981* ···

1981 年 1 月 4 日，万里长江第一坝——葛洲坝水利枢纽工程大江截流工程胜利合龙。图为 1981 年 1 月 4 日傍晚，大江截流正在紧张进行中

On January 4, 1981, the Gezhouba Water Conservancy Project, first of its kind on the Yangtze River, was successfully completed. The picture shows builders working hard for the closure of the river on the evening of January 4, 1981.

## ··· 1981 ···

1981年2月，全国总工会向全国青少年发出"五讲四美"活动倡议。几十年来，讲文明、讲礼貌、讲卫生、讲秩序、讲道德和心灵美、语言美、行为美、环境美的倡议已经成为青少年的文明礼貌准则。图为江苏省南京市长江路小学的少先队员们设立宣传站进行"五讲四美"宣传活动

In February 1981, the All-China Federation of Trade Unions called on adolescents throughout the country to stress decorum, good manners, hygiene, discipline and morals, as well as striving to improve the beauty of their minds, language, behavior and environment. The picture shows young pioneers of the Yangtze Road Primary School in Nanjing, Jiangsu Province setting up publicity stations.

## ··· *1981* ···

随着改革开放的不断深入，人们的生活发生了翻天覆地的变化。到了 20 世纪 80 年代，当年的老三大件，早已被电视机、冰箱、洗衣机取代。图为 1981 年，北京西单商场，群众抢购电视机

With the deepening of reform and opening up, people's lives underwent tremendous changes. In the 1980s, the original "three consumer items" had already been replaced by three new ones - TV sets, refrigerators and washing machines. The picture shows people buying TV sets in Beijing's Xidan Mall in 1981.

··· **1982** ···

1982 年 1 月，上海最大的理发店——南京理发店新添置了 26 台大型落地吹风机。这里每天接待 250 多名女顾客烫发，追求个性时尚蔚然成风

In January 1982, the Nanjing Hairdresser, largest barber shop in Shanghai, added 26 large-scale floor-mounted hair dryers. Here, where more than 250 female customers can receive daily perms, the pursuit of personality fashion prevails.

### ··· *1982* ···

1982 年 9 月，党的十二大明确将计划生育列为基本国策。图为河北省定县元光大队对领取独生子女光荣证的家庭给予表扬和奖励

In September 1982, the 12th National Congress of the CPC clearly listed family planning as a basic national policy. The picture shows Yuanguang Production Brigade in Dingxian County of Hebei Province rewarding families with a certificate of honor for having only child.

1982 年 12 月 4 日，五届全国人大五次会议通过并公布施行新的《中华人民共和国宪法》。这是新中国成立以来的第四部宪法。图为 12 月 5 日，上海第一百货商店的干部和职工在认真学习和讨论此宪法

On December 4, 1982, the Fifth Session of the Fifth National People's Congress adopted and promulgated the new Constitution of the People's Republic of China. This became the fourth constitution since the founding of the PRC in 1949. The picture shows managers and workers of Shanghai No.1 Department Store earnestly studying and discussing the new constitution on December 5.

**···1983···**

上海牌手表是 20 世纪七八十年代的名牌之一，在新中国成立后的三十几年里，一直是身份的象征，在 70 年代成为一代人的三大件之一。到了 80 年代，手表开始普及，越来越多的人开始佩戴手表。图为 1983 年 1 月 20 日，钟表降价的第一天，上海市钟表工业公司门市部的生意格外兴隆

The Shanghai brand watch was one of the famous brands in the 1970s and 1980s. It became a symbol of identity in the first three decades or so since the founding of the PRC, and one of the three major consumer items decided the 1970s generation. By the 1980s, watches became popular and more and more people began to wear them. The picture taken on January 20, 1983, first day of the price reduction of clocks and watches, shows business of the Shanghai Clocks and Watches Industry Co. looking particularly prosperous.

## ··· *1983* ···

在 20 世纪 80 年代，坐飞机还是一种新鲜的出行方式。当时，全国民航运输飞机 140 架，多数是四五十年代生产的型号。图为 1983 年 5 月，广东，梅县侨乡第一次降下民航飞机，吸引了群众围观

In the 1980s, taking a plane was a new way of traveling. At that time, 140 civil aviation transport aircraft were available, mostly produced in the 1940s and 1950s. The picture shows the first landing of a civil aircraft at Meixian Overseas Chinese Township, Guangdong Province in May 1983.

··· *1983* ···

1983 年 12 月 31 日，国务院召开第二次全国环境保护会议，明确提出环境保护是我国的一项基本国策。图为黑龙江省泰来县塔子城公社良种大队第三小队村民使用太阳能灶做饭，该村是全省第一个"新能源村"

On December 31, 1983, the State Council convened the Second National Conference on Environmental Protection, which clearly put forward that environmental protection was a basic national policy. The picture shows members of the Third Production Team of the Tazicheng People's Commune in Tailai County, Heilongjiang Province, using solar-powered cookers at home. The Third Production Team became the first "New Energy Village" in the province.

## ··· *1984* ···

1984 年 7 月 29 日，中国射击运动员
许海峰在第二十三届奥运会上为中国
夺得第一块金牌，打破了中国在奥运
会金牌榜上"零"的纪录。这也是这
届奥运会决出的第一块金牌

On July 29, 1984, Chinese shooter Xu
Haifeng won China's first ever Olympic gold
medal during the 23rd Olympic Games held
in Los Angeles, This broke China's record of
"zero" in the gold medal list of the Olympic
Games, which was also the first gold medal
decided in this LA Olympic Games.

## ··· *1984* ···

1984 年 10 月 1 日，参加国庆游行的大学生通过天安门城楼时，队伍展开"小平您好"的横幅。此画面瞬间传遍世界，成为共和国历史上珍贵的记忆

On October 1, 1984, as university students participating in the National Day parade passed before the Tian'anmen Rostrum in Beijing, the procession unfolded ae banner bearing words reading "Hi, Xiaoping", referring to Chinese leader Deng Xiaoping. This picture spread all over the world in an instant and became a precious memory in the history of the Republic.

··· *1984* ···

1984 年 12 月 19 日，中英两国政府在北京正式签署《中华人民共和国政府和大不列颠及北爱尔兰联合王国政府关于香港问题的联合声明》，确认中国政府将于 1997 年 7 月 1 日对香港恢复行使主权。图为香港居民聚集在湾仔一家电器行门前，观看中英关于香港问题的联合声明签字仪式的现场电视转播

On December 19, 1984, the Joint Declaration of the Government of the United Kingdom of Great Britain and Northern Ireland and the Government of the People's Republic of China on the Question of Hong Kong was formally signed in Beijing, confirming that the Chinese Government would resume the exercise of sovereignty over Hong Kong on July 1, 1997. The picture shows Hong Kong residents gathering in front of an electrical appliance store in Wanchai to watch a live television broadcast of the signing ceremony.

··· *1985* ···

1985 年 2 月 20 日，中国第一个南极考察站——长城站在南极乔治王岛建成。此后，我国又陆续建成南极中山站、昆仑站、泰山站

On February 20, 1985, the Great Wall Station, China's first Antarctic Research Station, was built on King George Island, Antarctica. Since then, China has built the Zhongshan Station, Kunlun Station and Taishan Station on the icy continent.

··· *1985* ···

1985 年 12 月，中国第一家地方国营航空公司——上海航空公司成立，图为空乘人员在上海飞往北京的航班上为乘客服务

Shanghai Airlines, China's first local state-owned airline, was established in December 1985. The picture shows flight attendants serving passengers on flights from Shanghai to Beijing.

**··· *1985* ···**

20 世纪 80 年代初期，喇叭裤、军大衣一度是时尚青年最喜爱的衣服。图为 1985 年，北京动物园门前，穿着喇叭裤、披着军大衣的时髦青年

Fashionable young people wearing bellbottoms and military overcoats in front of the Beijing Zoo in 1985. In the early 1980s, this formed the favorite costume of fashionable youth.

## ··· 1986 ···

1986 年 1 月 8 日，我国第二大汽车工业基地——第二汽车制造厂在湖北省十堰市建成投产。图为第二汽车制造厂生产的成批"东风"牌汽车准备出厂

On January 8, 1986, China's second largest automobile industry base, the Second Automobile Manufacturing Plant, was built and put into operation in Shiyan City, Hubei Province. The picture shows Dongfeng brand vehicles produced there ready to leave the factory.

··· *1986* ···

1986年9月13日，中国女子排球队在布拉格举行的第10届世界女子排球锦标赛上，以3比1战胜古巴队，成为第一支在世界女子排球大赛中获得五连冠的球队。中国女排完美地诠释了"女排精神"，激励和鼓舞了一代又一代人。图为中国女排队员在领奖台上向观众致意

On September 13, 1986, the Chinese Women's Volleyball Team defeated Cuba 3-1 in the 10th World Women's Volleyball Championship held in Prague, becoming the first team to win five consecutive championships in the event. The Chinese Women's Volleyball Team perfectly interpreted the spirit of women's volleyball, inspiring people of later generations. The picture shows the Chinese team saluting the audience on the podium.

## ··· *1987* ···

1987 年 4 月 13 日，中葡两国政府在北京正式签署《中华人民共和国政府和葡萄牙共和国政府关于澳门问题的联合声明》，确认中国政府于 1999 年 12 月 20 日对澳门恢复行使主权。图为中葡关于澳门问题的联合声明签字仪式结束后，港澳记者采访澳门知名人士

On April 13, 1987, in Beijing, the Chinese and Portuguese governments formally signed the Joint Statement between the Government of the People's Republic of China and the Government of the Portuguese Republic on Macao, confirming that the Chinese Government would resume the exercise of sovereignty over Macao on December 20, 1999. On the day of the signing, Hong Kong and Macao journalists interview Macao celebrities about the event.

··· *1987* ···

改革开放初期农副产品批发市场应运而生。图为 1987 年 5 月的北京大钟寺农贸市场

At the beginning of the reform and opening up program, the wholesale market of agricultural by-products emerged to meet the demands of the times. The picture shows the agricultural market of Dazhongsi in Beijing in May 1987.

···· *1987* ····

1987 年 11 月 12 日，北京前门，内地首家 "洋快餐" ——中美合资经营的 "北京美国肯德基家乡鸡快餐厅" 开始试营业。图为二楼餐厅一角

On November 12, 1987, Kentucky Fried Chicken, a typical American fast-food chain, began trial operation in Beijing. The Sino-American joint venture was also China's first Sino-foreign joint venture fast food restaurant in the country. The picture shows a corner of the second-floor restaurant.

1987 年 12 月 1 日，深圳经济特区启动全国首次国有土地使用权拍卖。图为深圳市政府在深圳会堂举行首次土地使用权公开拍卖

On December 1, 1987, the Shenzhen Special Economic Zone launched the first national auction of the right to use state-owned land. In the picture, the Shenzhen municipal government holds the first public auction of land use rights in Shenzhen Hall.

··· *1988* ···

1988年2月，国务院印发了《关于在全国城镇分期分批推行住房制度改革的实施方案》，改革鼓励职工买房，实现住房商品化。图为1988年8月，成都市亚光电工厂挂牌出售、出租新旧住房供职工选择的场景

In February 1988, the State Council issued the Implementation Plan for the Reform of the Housing System in Stages and Batches in Cities and Towns in the Country, encouraging employees to buy houses and help realize the commercialization of housing. In August 1988, the Chengdu Yaguang Factory sold or leased its dormitories among factory workers.

··· **_1988_** ···

1988 年 10 月 31 日，内地首条竣工的高速公路——沪嘉高速公路建成通车。到 2013 年
年底，中国高速公路通车总里程超过美国，位居世界第一

On October 31, 1988, the Hujia Expressway in Shanghai, the first short section of an expressway
on the Chinese mainland, was opened to traffic. By the end of 2013, the total mileage of China's
expressways exceeded the United States to rank first in the world.

··· *1988* ···

1988 年年底，贵州六盘水，市民最后一次排队领取肉票。自 1989 年 1 月起，全国取消"肉票"制度

At the end of 1988, in Liupanshui, Guizhou Province, citizens lined up for the last time to collect meat coupons. In January 1989, people in China began to buy meat at will, finally free of the old coupon system.

## *··· 1988 ···*

20 世纪 80 年代末期，随着生活水平的逐步提高，人们对生活品质的追求越来越强烈。当时许多大型家电，尤其是进口家电都是非常受欢迎的商品，往往供不应求。图为 1988 年，河南洛阳，市民在抢购冰箱

In the late 1980s, with the gradual improvement of living standards, the Chinese people developed a strong interest in the pursuit of a quality life. At that time, electrical household appliances, especially imported ones, were very popular. The picture shows people in Luoyang, Henan Province, rushing to buy refrigerators in 1988.

### 1989

1989 年 2 月 15 日，北京首批公开出售商品房登记第一天，共出售 350 套，房地产交易所的门还没开，已有上千人排起了队

On February 15, 1989, on the first day of registration for the first public sale of commercial housing in Beijing, 350 units were sold. The door of the real estate exchange has not yet opened, but thousands of people were already queuing.

··· *1989* ···

20世纪80年代末期至90年代初，开始流行一种具有保温功能的压力暖水瓶。在那时的上海，结婚时女方家里的嫁妆中若有压力暖水瓶，则证明这家人家的经济条件很好。图为1989年，上海第一百货商店保温瓶柜台前挤满了抢购新式保温瓶的人

From the late 1980s to the early 1990s, a kind of pressure thermos bottle with thermal insulation function began to gain popularity. In Shanghai, if there was a pressure thermos bottle in the dowry of the woman's family at the time of marriage, it proved that the family's economic condition was very good. The picture shows people rushing to buy new thermos bottles in front of a counter of Shanghai No.1 Department Store in 1989.

1990 年 9 月 22 日至 10 月 7 日，第十一届亚运会在北京举行，这是亚运会首次在中国举行。此后，2010 年第十六届亚运会在广州举办。图为第十一届亚运会开幕式，中国代表队入场

From September 22 to October 7, 1990, the 11th Asian Games were held in Beijing. This marked the first time China hosted the Games. In 2010, the 16th Asian Games was held in Guangzhou. The picture shows the Chinese sports delegation entering the stadium at the opening ceremony.

*··· 1990 ···*

自 1988 年海南建省办经济特区以后，大批建设特区的有识之士来到海南。"闯海人"的提法也是这一时期形成的，特指到海南岛开发建设和安家落户的大陆人。图为 1990 年 10 月，海口市新港码头，上海南岛的人蜂拥而至

Since the establishment of the Hainan Special Economic Zones in Hainan in 1988, large numbers of people have come to work in Hainan. The term "sea-breaker" came into being during this period, especially the mainlanders who developed and built Hainan Island and settled down. Picture shows the Haikou New Harbour Pier in October 1990, where people from the Shanghai South Island came.

1990 年 11 月 26 日，中国第一家证券交易所——上海证券交易所宣告成立并于 12 月中旬正式开业。图为上海证券交易所成立大会会场

On November 26, 1990, the Shanghai Stock Exchange, first of its kind in China, was established and officially opened in mid-December. The picture shows the Exchange's founding ceremony.

*…* ***1991*** *…*

1991 年 5 月 11 日，中国第一家高新技术交易市场——北京市新技术产业开发试验区科技贸易中心在中关村南部正式开业

On May 11, 1991, the Science and Technology Trade Center of the Beijing New Technology Industry Development Pilot Area, the first high-tech trading market in China, officially opened in the south of the Zhongguancun area of Beijing.

*··· 1991 ···*

1991 年 12 月 16 日，海峡两岸关系协会在北京正式成立。图为在人民大会堂台湾厅隆重举行的成立大会现场

On December 16, 1991, the Association for Relations Across the Taiwan Straits was formally established in Beijing. The picture shows the grand inauguration meeting held in the Taiwanese Hall of the Great Hall of the People in Beijing.

··· *1991* ···

1991 年 12 月，中国大陆第一座自行设计建造的核电站——浙江泰山核电站首次并网发电。它的建成，结束了中国大陆无核电的历史

In December 1991, the Zhejiang Qinshan Nuclear Power Station, first China-designed and China-constructed nuclear power plant on the mainland, was connected to the national grid for the first time. Its completion means China was finally making use of nuclear power.

··· **1992** ···

1992 年 12 月 1 日，新亚欧大陆桥（江苏连云港至荷兰鹿特丹铁路线）开通运营。它对环太平洋经济圈的协调发展起到重要作用，也使中国与世界大市场的距离更近。新亚欧大陆桥东端桥头堡江苏连云港在中国对外开放中具有特殊地位。图为大型滚装船正在连云港港口停靠，一批进口小轿车驶下巨轮

On December 1, 1992, the New Eurasian Continental Bridge (Lianyungang-Rotterdam Railway Line, Jiangsu Province) opened. It plays an important role in the coordinated development of the circum-Pacific economic circle, and also brings China closer to the world market. Lianyungang, Jiangsu Province, the eastern end of the New Eurasian Continental Bridge, has a special position of great economic significance in China's opening up. The picture shows a large ro-on/ro-off ship docking at Lianyungang Port to offload a shipment of imported cars.

## *1992*

1992 年，广东省宝安县的万丰村投资 300 万元，为全村 550 户农民装上了国内外程控直拨电话，成为内地第一个程控电话村

In 1992, Wanfeng Village, Shajing Town, Bao'an County, Guangdong Province, invested 3 million Yuan to install domestic and foreign program-controlled direct dial telephones for 550 farmers in the village. Wanfeng became the first program-controlled telephone village on the mainland.

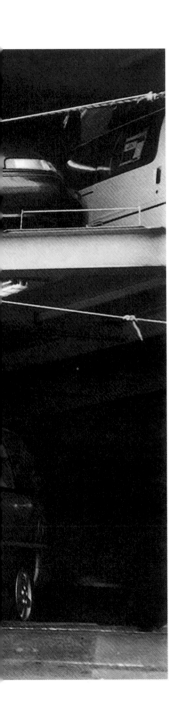

## ··· *1993* ···

中国与世贸组织的主要缔约方进行了长达3年的双边磋商，就中国复关的一些核心问题达成谅解。与此同时，中国与世界各经济体之间的交流与合作日益密切。图为1993年8月7日，1985辆雪佛兰汽车从美国运抵天津港，美方人员打出一幅写有"感谢你，中国"的横幅

China held bilateral consultations with major WTO parties for three years to reach an understanding on some core issues of China's customs clearance. At the same time, exchanges and cooperation between China and the world's economies became increasingly close. The picture shows 1,985 Chevrolet cars arriving at Tianjin Port from the United States on August 7, 1993. The American staff put out a banner with the words "Thank you, China".

··· *1993* ···

20 世纪 90 年代初期，通讯技术发展迅猛，BP 机、大哥大成了当时有钱人的象征。图为 1993 年，成都太升路自发形成的通讯一条街

In the early 1990s, communication modes developed rapidly. BP and cellular phones became the symbols of a rich life at that time. The picture shows a communications Equipment Street at Taisheng Road in Chengdu, Sichuan Province, in 1993.

外滙牌價表 OFFICIAL FOREIGN EXCHANGE QUOTATIONS 牌價單位:人民幣元
國家外滙管理總局 State Administration of Exchange Control RATE: IN RMB YUAN

## *I994*

1994 年 1 月 1 日，国务院决定改革现行汇率制度、实行人民币汇率并轨，我国开始实行以市场供求为基础的、单一的、有管理的浮动汇率制度。图为在北京贵友大厦外汇兑换处，外汇牌价表上显示 100 美元买价为人民币 867.83 元

On January 1, 1994, the State Council decided to reform the current exchange rate system and implement a merger of the RMB exchange rate. China began to implement a single, managed floating exchange rate system based on market supply and demand. The picture shows the Foreign Exchange Office at Guiyou Building in Beijing. The foreign exchange price list shows that the purchase price of US$100 is RMB 867.83.

**·· 1994 ··**

1994 年 8 月 19 日，中央国家机关首次招考公务员，录用名额为 490 人。图为考生在北京第四十四中学考区应试

On August 19, 1994, for the first time, central government organs recruited 490 civil servants through a unified exam system. The picture shows candidates taking the exam in Beijing No. 44 Middle School.

## ··· *1994* ···

1994 年，福建省厦门市金嶝商贸区首期工程破土动工。1999 年 5 月，厦门大嶝对台小额商品交易市场开业，这是大陆唯一的对台小额商品市场，极大地促进了两岸商贸往来

In 1994, the first phase of the Jindeng Commercial and Trade Zone in Xiamen City, Fujian Province, broke ground. In May 1999, Xiamen Dadeng opened the Small Commodity Exchange Market, sole mainland-to-Taiwan small commodity market to greatly promote cross-straits trade and commerce.

**··· 1995 ···**

1995年12月18日，我国第一条沙漠复线电气化铁路正式通车，该铁路穿越西北腾格里沙漠南缘的迎水桥至干塘。图为电力机车牵引着装满货物的货车奔驰在腾格里沙漠南缘的沙坡头地段

On December 18, 1995, the first desert double-track electrified railway was officially opened in China. The railway crosses Yingshui Bridge on the southern edge of the Tengger Desert in Northwest China to reach Gantang. The picture shows electric locomotives pulling trucks loaded with goods on the Shapotou section, along the southern edge of the Tengger Desert.

··· **1995** ···

20 世纪 90 年代，婚礼开始流行车队接亲。图为 1995 年，海南海口，用于婚礼的婚车

Wedding Cars were much in demand for weddings starting in the 1990s. The picture shows a wedding motorcade in Haikou, Hainan, in 1995.

**···1996···**

1996 年 9 月 1 日，京九铁路开通运营。京九铁路是当时中国国内投资最多、一次性建成的最长双线铁路，为中国"三横五纵"干线铁路网中的一纵

On September 1, 1996, the Beijing-Kowloon Railway was opened. At that time, the Beijing-Kowloon Railway was the longest double-tracked railway with the largest domestic investment and one-time construction. It formed part of the "Three Horizontal - Five Vertical" trunk railway network.

## ··· *1996* ···

1996 年 12 月 17 日，大亚湾核电站工程通过国家验收，正式交付生产运行。大亚湾核电站是中国大陆第一座引进外国资金、先进设备和技术建设的大型核电站，也是中国大陆第一座大型商业核电站

On December 17, 1996, the Daya Bay Nuclear Power Station passed national acceptance and was officially delivered for full operation. The Daya Bay Nuclear Power Station is the first large-scale nuclear power plants on the mainland, which introduced foreign capital and foreign advanced equipment and technology. It was also the first large-scale commercial nuclear power plant in China.

## ⋯ *1997* ⋯

1997 年 3 月 14 日，八届全国人大第五次会议决定，西南重镇重庆成为继北京、天津、上海之后的中国第四个直辖市。图为重庆夜景

On March 14, 1997, the Fifth Session of the Eighth National People's Congress decided that Chongqing, a key town in southwest China, would become the fourth municipality directly under the Central Government, after Beijing, Tianjin and Shanghai. The picture shows the night scene of Chongqing.

## ··· *1997* ···

1997 年 3 月 18 日，南昆铁路全线铺通。南昆铁路被称为"国家最大的扶贫项目"，是沟通西南与华南沿海的一条重要通道。图为布依族群众等候在位于贵州境内的八渡车站接轨点，想亲眼目睹铁路铺通的盛况

On March 18, 1997, the whole line of the Nanning-Kunming Railway was laid. Known as "the biggest poverty alleviation project of the country", it is an important channel to communicate with the coastal areas of South and Southwest China. The picture shows several Buyi ethnic minority people waiting at the junction of the Badu Station in Guizhou Province to witness the grand opening of the railway.

# ··· *1997* ···

1997 年 7 月 1 日零点，中国政府向世界宣布恢复对香港行使主权，成立中华人民共和国香港特别行政区。图为 1997 年 7 月 1 日清晨，在香港北角地铁站，一位乘客在阅读当天香港回归的报纸。地铁墙上挂着 1982 年中英谈判的大幅照片，也见证了当天的历史时刻

At 0:00 on July 1, 1997, the Chinese Government announced to the world that it would resume the exercise of sovereignty over Hong Kong and establish the Hong Kong Special Administrative Region of the People's Republic of China. The picture shows a passenger reading the newspaper on the day of Hong Kong returns to the embrace of the motherland at 6:00 a.m. on July 1, 1997 at the North Point Metro Station. On the wall of the metro are large photographs of the 1982 Sino-British negotiations, bearing witness to the historic moment.

## *··· 1997 ···*

1997 年 10 月 28 日，黄河小浪底水利枢纽工程截流成功，这是黄河治理历史上具有里程碑意义的水利工程。图为 8 车石料向狭窄的围堰龙口倾泻而下，黄河小浪底水利枢纽工程截流成功

On October 28, 1997, the Xiaolangdi Reservoir Project of the Yellow River, a landmark project in the history of national harnessing of the great waterway, was successfully closed. Here, eight trucks fully loaded with stone pour their loads down the narrow cofferdam, so that the Xiaolangdi Water Conservancy Project for the Yellow River was successfully closed.

··· *1998* ···

1998 年 7 月 3 日，国务院发出《关于进一步深化城镇住房制度改革 加快住房建设的通知》，提出从 1998 年下半年开始，全国城镇停止住房实物分配，逐步实行住房分配货币化。图为广州购房者在中介公司办理购房手续

On July 3, 1998, the State Council issued the Notice on Further Deepening the Reform of Urban Housing System and Accelerating Housing Construction. It was proposed that, starting from the second half of 1998, cities and towns throughout the country should stop housing distribution in kind and gradually implement monetization of housing distribution. The picture shows Guangzhou buyers going through the formalities of buying houses in the intermediary company.

··· *1998* ···

1998 年夏，长江流域发生了自 1954 年以来又一次全流域性大洪水，松花江流域嫩江出现超历史记录的特大洪水。图为 1998 年 8 月 8 日，江西省九江市，九江大堤决口第二天，战士们用身体挡住沙袋，以免被洪水冲走

In the summer of 1998, another catchment-wide flood occurred in the Yangtze River basin, and the Nenjiang River in the Songhua River basin experienced a catastrophic flood exceeding historical records. The picture shows Jiujiang City, Jiangxi Province, on August 8, 1998, the second day after a break occurred in the Jiujiang embankment. PLA soldiers worked tirelessly to ensure the sandbags weren't washed away by the flood.

*…1999…*

1999 年 9 月 28 日，横跨长江的江阴长江大桥竣工通车。江阴长江公路大桥是我国首座跨径超千米的特大型钢箱梁悬索桥梁，也是 20 世纪"中国第一、世界第四"的大钢箱梁悬索桥，代表我国造桥最高水平，是 20 世纪我国桥梁工程建设史上新的里程碑

On September 28, 1999, the Jiangyin Yangtze River Bridge across the Yangtze River was completed and opened to traffic. The Jiangyin Yangtze River Highway Bridge is the first super-large steel box girder suspension bridge with a span of over 1,000 meters in China. It is also the largest steel box girder suspension bridge in China and the fourth in the world in the 20th Century. It represents the highest level of bridge construction in China and is a new milestone in the history of bridge construction in China in the 20th Century.

## ··· *1999* ···

1999 年 12 月 20 日零时，北京，中国历史博物馆门前的澳门回归倒计时牌前，群众欢庆澳门回归

Mass celebration in front of the Museum of History in Beijing at 0:00 on December 20, 1999, as the countdown is completed for Macao's return to the motherland.

## *2000*

2000 年 3 月 2 日，中共中央、国务院发出《关于进行农村税费改革试点工作的通知》，要求通过试点，探索监理规范的农村税费制度和从根本上减轻农民负担的办法。图为山东省济阳县太平镇火炉村农户领取农补款

On March 2, 2000, the CPC Central Committee and the State Council issued the Notice on the Pilot Work of Tax and Fee Reform in Rural Areas, calling for exploration of a standardized rural tax and fee system under supervision, as well as ways to reduce farmers' burden fundamentally through the pilot work. The picture shows farmers in Huolu Village, Taiping Town, Jiyang County, Shandong Province receiving their agricultural subsidy.

···*2000*···

2000 年 6 月 29 日，南京军区"临汾旅"组织近千名党员开展"重温入党誓词，落实三个代表"活动，以增强部队全体党员爱党、爱国、爱军的意识

On June 29, 2000, the Linfen Brigade of the PLA Nanjing Military Region organized nearly 1,000 Party members to carry out the activity of "revisiting the oath of joining the Party and implementing the Three Representatives" in order to enhance the consciousness of patriotism of CPC, patriotism of the nation and patriotism of all members of the army.

2000 年 11 月 8 日上午，我国首批 "西电东送" 工程——洪家渡水电站、引子渡水电站、乌江渡水电站扩机工程同时开工。"西电东送" 是西部大开发的标志性工程。图为乌江洪家渡水电站开工典礼现场

On the morning of November 8, 2000, the first batch of "west-to-east power transmission" projects in China - Hongjiadu Hydropower Station, Yinzidu Hydropower Station and Wujiangdu Hydropower Station Expansion Project - started operating at the same time. "Power transmission from west to east" is a landmark project of Western China Development. The picture shows the opening ceremony of the Hongjiadu Hydropower Station on the Wujiang River.

··· **2001** ···

2001 年 4 月 3 日，教育部出台新政策，允许 25 周岁以上公民参加高考，彻底放开高校招生的年龄限制。图为江苏省南京市的 72 岁老人汪侠如愿以偿地拿到了高考准考证

On April 3, 2001, the Ministry of Education issued a new policy allowing citizens over 25 to take the college entrance examination, thus completely liberalizing the age limit for college enrollment. The picture shows Wang Xia, a 72-year-old man in Nanjing City, Jiangsu Province, who successfully obtained his college entrance examination pass.

··· *2001* ···

2001 年 7 月 13 日，2008 年奥运会主办城市投票结果揭晓——北京申奥成功。图为中央电视台内，群众庆祝申奥成功，挥动国旗的场景

On July 13, 2001, the host city of the 2008 Olympic Games was chosen, marking Beijing's successful bid. The picture from CCTV shows people celebrating the success and waving the national flag.

## ··· 2001 ···

2001 年 10 月 7 日，沈阳五里河体育场，在 2002 年世界杯预选赛中，中国男足 1 比 0 击败阿曼，首次打进世界杯 32 强

On October 7, 2001, at Wulihe Stadium in Shenyang, the Chinese Men's Football Team beat Oman 1-0 in 2002 World Cup qualifying match and reached the final stages of the World Cup for the first time.

*···* **2001** *···*

2001 年 11 月 10 日，世界贸易组织审议并通过了中国加入世贸组织的决定。图为外经贸部部长石广生举杯庆祝

On November 10, 2001, the WTO reviewed and adopted the decision allowing China to become a member. The picture shows Minister of Foreign Trade and Economic Cooperation Shi Guangsheng raising his glass to celebrate.

*··· 2002 ···*

2002年4月12日，首届博鳌亚洲论坛在海南博鳌开幕，来自中国、日本、韩国、泰国等48个国家和地区的政府官员、专家学者及企业界人士等2000人出席了年会

On April 12, 2002, the first Boao Forum for Asia opened in Boao, Hainan. A total of 2,000 government officials, experts, scholars and businessmen from 48 countries and regions, including China, Japan, South Korea and Thailand, attended.

··· *2002* ···

2002 年 12 月 3 日，在摩纳哥蒙特卡洛举行的国际展览局第一百三十二次成员国大会上，上海获得 2010 年世界博览会的举办权。图为申博结果宣布后，上海高校学生在南京路世纪广场欢呼雀跃

On December 3, 2002, Shanghai was awarded the right to host the 2010 World Expo, during the 132nd Congress of the International Exhibition Bureau held in Monte Carlo, Monaco. The announcement was greeted joyously by Shanghai university students at the Century Square on Nanjing Road.

"南水北调工程"主要解决我国北方地区，尤其是黄淮海流域的水资源短缺问题，规划区人口 4.38 亿人。2002 年 12 月 27 日，南水北调工程东线工程正式启动。图为江苏扬州宝应县，巨型铲挖机在"南水北调"东线工程潼河工地上投入施工

The South-to-North Water Diversion Project was launched to help solve the shortage of water resources in Northern China, especially in the Yellow-Huaihe-Haihe river basin, with a population of 438 million. On December 27, 2002, the East Route was officially launched. The picture shows in Baoying County, Yangzhou, Jiangsu Province, giant shovel excavators were put into construction at Tonghe construction site of the East Route Project of the South-to-North Water Diversion Project.

2003 年春节，广州 70% 的人家都到酒楼饭店吃年夜饭，许多酒楼饭店在大年三十晚上都要分两到三轮接待市民。随着生活水平的提高，人们对物质的要求越来越高，越来越多的家庭选择在饭店吃年夜饭

During the Spring Festival of 2003, an estimated 70% of people in Guangzhou went to restaurants for their Lunar New Year's dinner. Many restaurants have two or three rounds of reception for the public on the evening of lunar New Year's Eve. With the improvement of living standards, public material requirements are getting higher and higher. More and more families choose to eat the Lunar New Year's Eve dinner in restaurants rather than at home.

## ··· *2003* ···

2003 年 2 月 27 日，悬挂在天安门广场东侧的"中国历史博物馆"和"中国革命博物馆"摘牌。次日，"中国国家博物馆"挂牌。这意味着，由历博、革博合并组成的中国国家博物馆正式成立

On February 28, 2003, the Museum of Chinese History and the Museum of Chinese Revolution on the east side of Tian'anmen Square merged to become the National Museum of China.

### ··· *2003* ···

2003 年春天，我国遭遇了一场非典型肺炎疫情重大灾害。全党全国人民在中共中央、国务院的领导下夺取了防治非典工作的阶段性重大胜利。图为 2003 年 5 月 6 日，一对新婚夫妇穿过街道时戴着口罩以防非典

In the spring of 2003, China suffered a severe SARS epidemic. Under the leadership of the CPC Central Committee and the State Council, the whole country won a major victory in the prevention and control of SARS. Here a newly-married couple wearing a surgical mask for protection cross the street on May 6, 2003.

2004 年 1 月 6 日上午，中国首条双圆隧道在上海胜利贯通。这条双圆隧道全长 2688 米。中国是继日本之后、世界上第二个掌握双圆隧道施工技术的国家。图为建设者们在欢呼庆祝

On the morning of January 6, 2004, China's first double circular tunnel, 2,688 meters long, was successfully connected in Shanghai. China is the second country in the world to master this complex construction technology after Japan. The picture shows tunnel workers celebrating.

*2004*

2004 年 12 月 30 日，线路总长约 4000 公里的"西气东输工程"一线工程全线投产并正式开始商业运营。"西气东输工程"是仅次于长江三峡工程的又一重大投资项目，是拉开"西部大开发"序幕的标志性建设工程。图为西气东输终点站上海白鹤站

On December 30, 2004, the first-line project of the West-to-East Gas Transmission Project, with a total length of about 4000 kilometers, went into operation and formally started commercial operation. This is another major investment project second only to the Three Gorges Dam Project of the Yangtze River. It is also a landmark construction project as a prelude to work on Western China's development. The picture shows the Shanghai Baihe Station, terminal of the gas pipeline.

*··· 2005 ···*

2005 年 1 月 18 日，中国南极内陆冰盖昆仑科考队确认找到了南极内陆冰盖的最高点。这是人类首次踏上南极内陆冰盖最高点。图为 2005 年 1 月 8 日，中国第二十一次南极科考队队员在南极开凿冰面进行科学考察

On January 18, 2005, the Kunlun Science Research Team of China's Antarctic Inland Ice Sheet confirmed the discovery of the highest point of the Antarctic Inland Ice Sheet. This was the first time humans had reached this point. The picture shows the 21st Antarctic Science Expedition team of China digging ice on January 8, 2005.

*…* **2005** *…*

2005年3月5日至14日，十届全国人大三次会议召开，通过《反分裂国家法》。图为同年3月5日，在澳大利亚悉尼举行的澳大利亚中国统一促进会成立大会上，会员们展示支持中国制定反分裂国家法的签名

From March 5 to 14, 2005, the Third Session of the 10th National People's Congress was held, passing the Anti-Secession Law. The picture shows signatures of the members supporting China's anti-secession law at the inaugural meeting of the Australian Association for the Promotion of Chinese Unification held in Sydney on March 5.

天津 二 长沙 二 昆明

*2005*

2005 年 3 月 11 日，中国内地首家民营航空公司——奥凯航空公司的首次航班 BK2811 顺利抵达昆明。图为机组人员在昆明机场合影

On March 11, 2005, the first flight BK2811 of the Okay Airways Co., Ltd., the first private airline on the Chinese mainland, arrived in Kunming. The picture shows the crew taking a group photo at Kunming Airport.

**2006**

2006 年 1 月 31 日，国务院发出《关于解决农民工问题的若干意见》，提出保障农民工合法权益的政策体系和执法监督机制、惠及农民工的城乡公共服务体制和制度。图为 1 月 24 日，在贵阳市打工的农民工领取 2005 年的工资

On January 31, 2006, the State Council issued the Opinions on Solving the Problem of Migrant Workers, putting forward a systemic policy, law enforcement measures and supervisory mechanism to safeguard the legitimate rights and interests of migrant workers, as well as the urban and rural public service system and system also of great benefit to migrant workers. The picture, taken on January 24, 2006, shows migrant workers in Guiyang, Guizhou Province, receiving wages not paid in 2005.

**··· *2006* ···**

2006 年 5 月 20 日，三峡工地雨后初晴，全线浇筑到顶的三峡大坝展现新姿。三峡水电站的主体工程是当今世界最大的水利发电工程

The whole concrete project of the Three Gorges Dam, the largest hydropower project in the world, showing a new look after rain on May 20, 2006.

## ··· *2006* ···

2006 年 7 月 1 日，青藏铁路全线通车。
青藏铁路是世界上海拔最高、线路最长
的铁路线路

On July 1, 2006, the Qinghai-Tibet Railway,
longest railway line with the highest altitude
in the world, opened to traffic.

## *2006*

2006 年 12 月 22 日，华晨汽车集团控股有限公司 3000 辆中华尊驰轿车运抵大连，通过大连港发往德国不来梅。此批轿车为华晨与德国 HSO 公司签署的 15.8 万辆中的首批，也是中国自主品牌汽车首次大批量出口欧洲。图为准备运往欧洲的中华轿车

On December 22, 2006, 3,000 China Zunchi cars of the Huachen Automotive Group Co., Ltd. arrived in Dalian for shipment to Bremen, Germany, through the Dalian Port. This is the first batch of 158,000 cars manufactured according to the contract signed by Huachen and German HSO Co. It is also the first batch of Chinese self-owned brand cars exported to Europe. The picture shows Chinese cars ready for shipment to Europe.

··· *2007* ···

2007 年 7 月 11 日，国务院发出通知
在全国建立农村最低生活保障制度，
以切实解决农村贫困人口的生活困
难。图为 8 月 31 日，广西南丹县里
湖乡甲木村低保户在里湖乡民政办公
室领到城乡最低生活保障金领取证

On July 11, 2007, the State Council decreed
the establishment of a rural minimum living
security system throughout the country in
order to effectively solve the living difficulties
of rural poor. Taken on August 31, the
picture shows low-income households in
Jiamu Village, Lihu Township, Nandan
County, Guangxi Zhuang Autonomous
Region, receiving their minimum living
allowance certificates from the Lihu
Township Civil Affairs Office.

## ··· *2007* ···

2007 年 10 月 2 日，2007 年夏季世界特殊奥林匹克运动会在上海体育场盛大开幕。这
是此项国际赛事首次在中国举办。图为开幕式现场

On October 2, 2007, the 2007 Summer World Special Olympic Games opened in the Shanghai
Stadium. This is the first time fort this international event to be held in China. The picture shows
the opening ceremony.

**··· 2007 ···**

2007 年 10 月 24 日，我国第一颗探月卫星"嫦娥一号"在西昌发射中心成功升空，标志着我国首次探月工程取得圆满成功。探月工程是我国继人造地球卫星、载人航天之后，航天活动的第三个里程碑

On October 24, 2007, Chang'e-1, China's first lunar exploration satellite, was successfully launched from Xichang Satellite Launch Center in Sichuan Province. It marks the success of China's initial lunar exploration project. Lunar exploration is the third milestone of Chinese space activities after development of an artificial Earth satellite and manned spaceflight.

··· **2007** ···

2007 年 12 月 14 日，国务院发布关于修改《全国年节及纪念日放假办法》的决定。从 2008 年起，五一劳动节从放假 3 天减为 1 天，增设清明、端午、中秋三个假期。图为 2008 年 10 月 1 日，游客在上海南京路步行街参加国庆观灯活动

On December 14, 2007, the State Council issued a decision on amending the Holiday Measures for New Year Festival and Memorial Days. Since 2008, May Day has been reduced from a three-day to a single day break, with three additional holidays added including the Qingming Festival, Dragon Boat Festival and Mid-Autumn Festival. The picture shows tourists taking part in the National Day Lantern Festival in the Nanjing Road Pedestrian Street in Shanghai on October 1.

### ··· *2008* ···

2008 年年初，我国南方部分地区遭遇严重低温雨雪冰冻灾害。图为南方电网公司组织人力进行线路抢修

At the beginning of 2008, parts of Southern China suffered from severe cold, snow and ice. The picture shows workers of China Southern Power Grid Corporation undertaking emergency repairs.

### ··· 2008 ···

2008 年 5 月 12 日，四川省汶川县发生里氏 8.0 级地震，地震共造成 69227 人死亡，374643 人受伤，17923 人失踪，是新中国成立以来破坏力最大的地震。经国务院批准，自 2009 年起，每年 5 月 12 日为全国"防灾减灾日"。图为从废墟中营救出来的儿童向解放军叔叔敬礼表示感谢

On May 12, 2008, a magnitude 8 earthquake struck Wenchuan County, Sichuan Province. The earthquake caused 69,227 deaths, injured 374,643 persons and left 17,923 missing. It was the most devastating earthquake since the founding of the PRC in 1949. With the approval of the State Council, from 2009 onwards, May 12 has become National Disaster Prevention and Mitigation Day. The picture shows a child rescued from the ruins saluting his PLA benefactors.

## ··· *2008* ···

2008 年 8 月 1 日，我国第一条具有自主
知识产权、国际一流水平的高速城际铁
路——京津城际铁路正式开通运营。这
是中国第一条时速 350 公里的高速铁路。
图为我国首列和谐号动车组列车飞驰在
京津城际铁路天津境内杨村特大桥上

On August 1, 2008, the Beijing-Tianjin
Intercity Railway, China's first high-
speed inter-city railway with independent
intellectual property rights and displaying
a world-class level, was officially opened.
Trains travel at an average 350 kph. The
picture shows the first Harmony EMU train
speeding across Yangcun Bridge in Tianjin.

## ··· *2008* ···

2008 年 8 月 8 日晚，第二十九届北京
奥运会开幕式在国家体育场隆重举行。
在本届奥运会上，中国以 51 枚金牌居
金牌榜首位，是奥运历史上首个登上金
牌榜榜首的亚洲国家。图为开幕式上的
焰火表演

On the evening of August 8, 2008, the
opening ceremony of the 29th Beijing
Olympic Games was solemnly held in the
National Stadium in Beijing. The host nation
celebrated by ranking first with 51 gold
medals, the first Asian country to top the
gold medal table in Olympic history. The
picture shows the fireworks show at the
opening ceremony.

··· **2008** ···

2008 年 12 月 15 日，两岸"三通"正式启动。海峡两岸分别在北京、天津、上海、福州、深圳以及台北、高雄、基隆等城市同时开通海上直航、空中直航以及直接通邮。两岸"三通"迈开历史性步伐。图为当日，旅客正通过东航的专用通道办理登机手续

On December 15, 2008, the two sides of the Taiwan Straits held commencement and celebration ceremonies of direct navigation by sea, air and direct mail in Beijing, Tianjin, Shanghai, Fuzhou, Shenzhen, Taipei, Kaohsiung and Keelung, a historic step. The picture shows passengers were checking in via a special passageway of China Eastern Airlines.

## *··· 2009 ···*

2009 年 3 月 28 日，西藏举行首次百万农奴解放纪念日庆祝大会。此前，1 月 19 日，西藏自治区九届人大二次会议通过决议，决定每年 3 月 28 日为西藏百万农奴解放纪念日。图为当日，藏族群众在庆祝大会现场

On March 28, 2009, Tibet held its first celebration of the anniversary of the emancipation of a million of serfs. Earlier, on January 19, the Second Session of the Ninth Tibet People's Congress adopted a resolution to make March 28 each year the anniversary of the Tibetan Serfs' Emancipation Day in Tibet. The picture shows Tibetan people celebrating.

**··· 2009 ···**

2009 年 4 月 29 日，国务院发出《关于推进上海加快发展现代服务业和先进制造业 建设国际金融中心和国际航运中心的意见》，明确将上海建设成为国际金融中心、国际航运中心和现代国际化大都市。图为上海外滩夜景

On April 29, 2009, the State Council issued the Opinions on Promoting Shanghai to Accelerate the Development of Modern Service Industry and Advanced Manufacturing Industry to Build an International Financial Center and an International Shipping Center, which clearly established Shanghai as an international financial center, an international shipping center and a modern international metropolis. The picture shows a night view of Shanghai Bund.

··· *2010* ···

2010 年 1 月 1 日，中国—东盟自由贸易区正式全面启动。关税的降低将使商品更容易地走进双方市场，让普通百姓享受到更多的实惠。图为 1 月 1 日，在广西省南宁市最大的果蔬批发市场——五里亭果蔬批发市场，市民在选购来自东盟各国的水果

On January 1, 2010, the China-ASEAN Free Trade Area was officially launched in an all-round way. The reduction of tariffs makes it easier for commodities to enter the markets of both sides, and allows ordinary people to enjoy more benefits. The picture taken on January 1, shows the scene of Wuliting, largest fruit and vegetable wholesale market in Nanning, Guangxi Zhuang Autonomous Region, people select exotic fruits from ASEAN countries.

···*2010*···

2010 年 3 月，第一次全国对口支援新疆工作会议召开。图为 2010 年 7 月 1 日，由河北省对口支援新疆生产建设兵团、总投资 4515.2 万元的"河北现代农业研发基地"在新疆兵团农二师 29 团开工奠基

In March 2010, the first National Working Conference on Counterpart Support to Xinjiang was held in Beijing. The picture shows the foundation stone-laying ceremony held for the 29th Regiment of the Second Agricultural Division of Xinjiang Production and Construction Corps (XPCC) on July 1, 2010. The project was to be undertaken with 45.152 million Yuan from the Hebei Modern Agricultural Research and Development Base of Hebei Province.

### ··· *2010* ···

第四十一届世界博览会于 2010 年 5 月 1 日至 10 月 31 日，在上海举行。本次世博会是由中国举办的首届世界博览会，是参展规模、园区面积最大的世博会。图为 2010 年 4 月 30 日晚，上海世博会开幕式的大型灯光喷泉焰火表演

The 41st World Expo was held in Shanghai from May 1 to October 31, 2010. This is the first World Expo held by China, and is the largest Expo in terms of scale and area. The picture shows a large-scale lighted fountain fireworks display at the opening ceremony on the evening of April 30, 2010.

2010 年 6 月 29 日，海峡两岸关系协会与台湾海峡交流基金会在重庆签署海峡两岸经济合作框架协议》。图为 7 月 17 日，高雄县六龟乡茬浓村种植芒果的苏文龙一家在院子里将刚刚收获的芒果装箱准备销往大陆

On June 29, 2010, the Association for Relations Across the Taiwan Straits and the Taiwan Strait Exchange Foundation signed the Framework Agreement on Cross-Strait Economic Cooperation in Chongqing. The picture shows Su Wenlong's family of Laonong Village, Liugui Township in Taiwan's Kaohsiung County, packing newly harvested mango fruit in their yard for sale to the mainland on July 17.

··· *2010* ···

2010 年 10 月 28 日，十一届全国人大常委会第十七次会议通过《中华人民共和国社会保险法》。这是我国最高国家立法机关首次就社保制度进行立法。图为山东省临沂市郯城县城乡居民社会养老保险服务大厅工作人员在展示城乡居民社会养老保险缴费证

On October 28, 2010, the 17th Session of the Standing Committee of the 11th National People's Congress passed the Social Insurance Law of the People's Republic of China. This is the first time China's supreme national legislature legislated on the social security system. The picture shows staff of the social endowment insurance service hall of urban and rural residents in Tancheng County, Linyi City, Shandong Province, displaying social endowment insurance payment certificates.

2010 年 12 月 12 日，国务院办公厅发布《关于开展国家教育体制改革试点的通知》，标志我国教育体制改革试点全面启动。图为 4 月 20 日，到秦皇岛东港镇第二小学支教的果艳丽在给孩子们上音乐课

On December 12, 2010, the General Office of the State Council issued the Notice on the Pilot Reform of the National Educational System, marking full-scale launch of the pilot reform of the country's educational system. The picture shows Guo Yanli, a teacher at No. 2 Primary School of Donggang Town, Qinhuangdao, giving music lessons to children on April 20.

2011 年 2 月 15 日，全国深化医药卫生体制改革工作会议在北京召开，部署拓展公立医院改革试点，建立健全基本药物制度，努力实现全民基本医保等措施。图为 2 月 18 日居民在江苏海安县医疗保险基金管理中心办理医保结算报销业务

On February 15, 2011, the National Conference on Deepening Reform of the Medical and Health System was held in Beijing. The pilot projects for the reform of public hospitals were deployed, the basic drug system was established and improved, and efforts were made to achieve universal basic medical insurance. The picture taken on February 18, shows residents of Hai'an County, Jiangsu Province, handling the medical insurance settlement and reimbursement business at the Medical Insurance Fund Management Center.

··· *2011* ···

2011 年 2 月 22 日至 3 月 5 日，因利比亚国内形势发生重大变化，中国政府分批组织中国在利比亚人员 35860 人次安全有序撤离。这是新中国成立以来中国政府最大规模的有组织撤离海外中国公民的行动。图为中国军队协助利比亚撤侨行动

From February 22 to March 5, 2011, the Chinese Government organized the safe and orderly evacuation of 35,860 Chinese personnel in Libya in batches due to major changes in the domestic situation. This is the largest organized evacuation of overseas Chinese citizens by the Chinese Government since the founding of the PRC. In the picture, the Chinese army assist the evacuation of Libyan nationals.

2011 年 11 月 10 日，我国政府承诺当年建设的 1000 万套保障房全部开工。图为 10 月 27 日位于上海浦江镇的一处在建保障房工地

On November 10, 2011, the Chinese Government promised to start construction of 10 million units of security housing immediately. The picture shows the construction site of a security house project in Pujiang Town, Shanghai, on October 27.

## *···* **2011** *···*

2011 年 12 月 1 日，我国对外公布了《中国农村扶贫开发纲要（2011—2020 年）》，向贫困发起新一轮 "攻坚战"。这是我国第三次针对扶贫制订国家级规划。图为拉萨市当雄县纳木湖乡牧民达瓦次仁的孩子在新房内展示玩具。他家被纳入西藏农牧民安居工程

On December 1, 2011, China published the Outline of China's Rural Poverty Alleviation and Development (2011-2020), launching a new round of the "battle against poverty". This is the third time China has formulated a national plan for poverty alleviation. The picture shows the children of Dawa Chiren, a herdsman in Namtso Township, Damxung County, Lhasa, who have been included in the Tibetan farmer-herdsman housing project.

··· *2012* ···

2012 年 6 月 18 日、24 日，"神舟九号"载人飞船与"天宫一号"目标飞行器先后成功进行自动交会对接和航天员手控交会对接。图为 6 月 18 日拍摄的北京航天飞控中心大屏幕显示的"神舟九号"飞船与"天宫一号"交会对接的画面

On June 18 and 24, 2012, Shenzhou-9 manned spacecraft and Tiangong-1 target spacecraft successfully carried out a rendezvous and manual docking with astronauts. The picture shows the rendezvous and docking of Shenzhou-9 spacecraft and Tiangong-1 on the large screen of Beijing Aerospace Flight Control Center on June 18.

*… 2012 …*

2012 年 6 月 27 日，"蛟龙号"载人潜水器最大下潜深度达到 7062 米，创造了世界同类型载人潜水器下潜新纪录，这表明我国海底载人科学研究和资源勘探能力达到国际领先水平。图为 30 日下午 5 时 42 分，"蛟龙号"被吊起收回"向阳红九号"母船

On June 27, 2012, the Jiaolong manned submersible reached a maximum depth of 7,062 meters, creating a new world record for this type of manned submersible. China's seabed manned scientific research and resource exploration capabilities thus reached the international leading level. The picture taken at 5:42 p.m. on June 30, Jiaolong was being retrieved by the mother ship Xiangyanghong 9.

··· *2012* ···

2012 年 7 月 24 日上午 10 时 40 分，海南省三沙市成立大会暨揭牌仪式在三沙市永兴岛隆重举行。三沙市是我国最南端的地级行政区，同时也是全国总面积最大、陆地面积最小、人口最少的城市。图为 7 月 24 日揭牌仪式结束后拍摄的三沙市委市政府大楼

On July 24, 2012, at 10:40 a.m., the inauguration and unveiling ceremony of Sansha City, Hainan Province, was solemnly held at Yongxing Island, Sansha City. This is the southernmost prefectural-level administrative city in China. It is also the city with the largest total area, the smallest land area and the smallest population. The picture shows the building housing the Sansha city government and Sansha Party committee after the unveiling ceremony on July 24.

··· **2012** ···

2012 年 10 月 11 日，中国作家莫言获得 2012 年诺贝尔文学奖，正在德国法兰克福举行的国际书展上掀起一股莫言热。图为当日，在德国法兰克福国际书展上，摄影记者拍摄莫言小说《檀香刑》德文版

On October 11, 2012, Chinese writer Mo Yan gained the Nobel Prize for Literature, prompting huge interest in his works at the Frankfurt Book Fair in Germany. Photographers take pictures of the German version of Moyan's novel *Sandalwood Penalty*.

# 第三章 强起来
## Chapter III China Becomes Strong

党的十八大以来，在以习近平同志为核心的党中央领导下，在新中国成立特别是改革开放以来我国发展取得的重大成就基础上，党和国家事业发生历史性变革、取得历史性成就，中国特色社会主义进入了新时代。

进入新时代，我国经济建设取得重大成就，经济保持中高速增长，在世界主要国家中名列前茅；全面深化改革取得重大突破，主要领域改革主体框架基本确立；民主法治建设迈出重大步伐；扶贫攻坚续写了世界瞩目的中国"减贫奇迹"，社会保障制度不断完善，受惠群体不断扩大；中华民族伟大复兴的中国梦和社会主义核心价值观深入人心；坚持"保护生态环境就是保护生产力，改善生态环境就是发展生产力"的绿色发展理念，资源利用效率不断提升，生态环境明显改善……

进入新时代，我国社会主要矛盾已经转化为人民日益增长的美好生活需要和不平衡不充分的发展之间的矛盾，经济发展已从高速增长阶段转向高质量发展阶段。

进入新时代，全面建设社会主义现代化国家的新征程已经开启，近代以来久经磨难的中华民族迎来了从站起来、富起来到强起来的伟大飞跃，迎来了实现中华民族伟大复兴的光明前景。

Since the 18th National Congress of the CPC, on the basis of the great achievements the PRC has made since its founding in 1949, and especially since the reform and opening-up beginning in late 1978, the cause of the CPC and the State has undergone historic changes and achieved notable achievements, and socialism with Chinese characteristics has entered a new era.

China has maintained moderate to high-speed economic growth in the new era, ranking among the leading countries in the world; major breakthroughs have been made in deepening reform in an all-round way, and the main framework of reform in major areas has been basically established; major steps have been taken in the construction of democracy and the rule of law; and the poverty alleviation campaign has continued to create the world-famous "miracle of poverty reduction" and creation of an all-embracing social security system has been constantly improved to benefit a constantly expanding number of people; the Chinese dream of the great rejuvenation of the Chinese nation and the socialist core values are deeply rooted in the hearts of the people; the green development concept of "protecting the ecological environment means protecting productivity, and improving the ecological environment means developing productivity" is being strongly promoted and widely accepted, the efficiency of resource utilization is constantly improving, and the ecological environment is obviously improved.

In the new era, the main social contradiction has been transformed into the contradiction between the people's growing need for a better life and unbalanced and inadequate development. Economic development has shifted from high-speed growth to high-quality development.

A new journey has begun to build a socialist modern country in an all-round way. In modern times, the Chinese nation, which had greatly suffered for a long time, has been able to usher in a great leap forward from simply standing up, to getting rich, and to becoming strong, leading to the present bright prospects for realizing a great national rejuvenation.

**2012**

2012年11月8日至14日，中国共产党第十八次全国代表大会举行。此次大会对我们党团结带领全国各族人民继续全面建设小康社会、加快推进社会主义现代化、开创中国特色社会主义事业新局面具有重大而深远的意义。11月15日，十八届一中全会选举习近平为中央委员会总书记。图为在复旦大学多媒体教室，同学们在观看党的新一届领导集体亮相的直播

From November 8 to 14, 2012, the 18th CPC National Congress was held. This was of great and far-reaching significance for the CPC to unite and lead the Chinese people of all ethnic groups to continue to build a well-off society in an all-round way, accelerate socialist modernization and create a new situation for the cause of socialism with Chinese characteristics. Xi Jinping was elected General Secretary of the CPC Central Committee at the First Plenary Session of the 18th National CPC Congress on November 15. The picture shows students of Fudan University watching the live broadcast of the new leading group of the Party in the university's multimedia classroom.

··· **2013** ···

2013年1月26日，我国自主发展的运-20大型运输机首次试飞取得圆满成功。运-20大型运输机的首飞成功，对于推进我国经济和国防现代化建设具有重要意义。图为运-20大型运输机在进行试飞

On January 26, 2013, China carried out its first successful test of the self-developed Yun-20 large transport aircraft. The success was of great significance to the modernization of China's economy and national defense. The picture shows the test flight.

··· *2013* ···

2013年8月，国务院正式批准设立中国（上海）自由贸易试验区。图为9月10日，中国（上海）自由贸易试验区洋山保税港区洋山港集装箱码头

In August 2013, the State Council formally approved the establishment the China (Shanghai) Free Trade Pilot Zone. The picture shows the Yangshan Port Container Terminal, Yangshan Bonded Port Area of the China (Shanghai) Free Trade Pilot Area on September 10.

祝贺宁夏·哈萨克斯坦国际货运包机正式通

**⋯ 2013 ⋯**

2013年9月7日，习近平在哈萨克斯坦纳扎尔巴耶夫大学发表演讲，提出共同建设"丝绸之路经济带"的倡议。图为2014年1月11日，在宁夏银川河东国际机场举行的银川—哈萨克斯坦货运直航包机通航仪式

On September 7, 2013, Xi Jinping delivered a speech at Nazarbayev University in Kazakhstan, proposing to jointly build the Silk Road Economic Belt. The picture shows the opening ceremony to mark direct freight charter flights between Yinchuan and Kazakhstan, held at Hedong International Airport in Yinchuan of Ningxia Hui Autonomous Region.

## ··· *2013* ···

2013 年 10 月 2 日至 8 日，习近平对印度尼西亚、马来西亚进行国事访问时，提出共同建设"21 世纪海上丝绸之路"的倡议。中国境内海上丝绸之路主要有广州、泉州、宁波三个主港和其他支线港组成。图为浙江宁波港集装箱码头

During his State visit to Indonesia and Malaysia from October 2 to 8, 2013, President Xi Jinping put forward an initiative to jointly build the Marine Silk Road for the 21st Century. The Marine Silk Road in China is mainly composed of three main ports including Guangzhou, Quanzhou and Ningbo, and other branch ports. The picture shows the container terminal of the Beilun Chuanshan Port Area in Ningbo Port, Zhejiang Province on January 18, 2015.

### ··· **2013** ···

2013 年 10 月 31 日，西藏墨脱公路正
式通车，墨脱成为我国最后一个通公路
的县。至此，我国实现了"县县通公路"
的目标。图为墨脱公路

On October 31, 2013, the Medog Highway
in Tibet was officially opened to traffic,
meaning there were no longer any counties
in China without access to highways.

## ··· *2013* ···

2013 年 11 月，我国第一艘航空母舰 "辽宁舰" 从青岛赴中国南海展开为期 47 天的海上综合演练，标志着 "辽宁舰" 开始具备海上编队战斗群能力。图为 "辽宁舰" 在海上航行

In November 2013, the first aircraft carrier Liaoning sailed from Qingdao to the South China Sea for a 47-day comprehensive drill at sea, marking that *Liaoning* possesses the capability of marine formation battle group. The picture shows Liaoning sailing at sea.

··· **2013** ···

2013 年 12 月 15 日，"嫦娥三号"着陆器和巡视器"玉兔号"月球车互拍成像。我国探月工程第二步战略目标圆满完成，成为世界上第三个月球软着陆和巡视探测的国家。图为北京飞控中心大屏幕上显示的"嫦娥三号"探测器正在着陆

On December 15, 2013, the Chang'e-3 lander and the Yutu lunar rover photograph each other. The second strategic goal of China's lunar exploration project was successfully accomplished, making China the third country in the world to achieve a soft landing and undertake exploration of the moon. The picture shows the Chang'e-3 probe landing on the big screen of the Beijing Flight Control Center.

··· *2014* ···

2014 年 2 月，十二届全国人大常委会第七次会议决定将 9 月 3 日确定为中国人民抗日战争胜利纪念日，将 12 月 13 日设立为南京大屠杀死难者国家公祭日。图为 2014 年 12 月 13 日，首个国家公祭日活动在侵华日军南京大屠杀遇难同胞纪念馆举行

In February 2014, the Seventh Session of the 12th NPC Standing Committee decided to designate September 3 as the anniversary of the victory in the Chinese people's War of Resistance against Japan, and December 13 as the National Memorial Day for the Victims of the Nanjing Massacre. The picture shows on December 13, 2014, China opened its first National Memorial Day in the Memorial Hall of the Victims in Nanjing Massacre by Japanese Invaders.

··· **2014** ···

2014年4月18日，林场工人在塞罕坝机械林场千层板林场苗圃内挑选樟子松树苗。他们用青春、汗水、智慧甚至血肉之躯同土地沙化顽强抗争，营造起112万亩森林，创造了世界上面积最大的人工林奇迹

On April 18, 2014, workers select camphor pine trees seedlings in the nursery of Thousand-ply Forest Farm of the Saihanba Mechanical Forest Farm. Through great efforts, they were able to establish 74,667 hectares of forest, creating the largest artificial forest miracle in the world.

··· **2014** ···

2014年11月，国家旅游局发布的数据显示，中国内地公民当年出境旅游首次突破1亿人次。从"请进来"到"走出去"，中国内地公民出境旅游人数自有统计数据的1998年的843万人次，到2014年破亿，增长了10.8倍，这是中国旅游业发展的一个里程碑，也是中国改革开放、经济社会发展进入新阶段具有标志性意义的大事。图为2014年11月，广州市一家旅行社举行春节境外游热卖会

According to released data from the China National Tourism Administration in November 2014, the number of outbound tours by Chinese mainland citizens exceeded 100 million for the first time. Statistics show the number of outbound tours used by Chinese mainland citizens was 8.43 million in 1998, the first year for which figures were available, but this shot up to 100 million in 2014, a 10.8-fold increase. This was hailed as a great achievement for the successful reform and opening-up. The picture shows a travel agency in Guangzhou staging an overseas tour promotion sale for the approaching Spring Festival.

**···2014···**

2014 年 11 月 17 日，上海与香港股票市场交易互联互通机制"沪港通"正式启动。"沪港通"是中国资本市场对外开放的重要内容，有利于加强两地资本市场联系，推动资本市场双向开放。图为山东省青岛市，股民在证券交易厅观看沪港通宣传板

On November 17, 2014, the Shanghai-Hong Kong Stock Exchanges Connectivity Mechanism was officially launched. "Shanghai-Hong Kong Stock Connect" is an important part of China's capital market opening to the outside world, conducive to strengthening the capital market links between the two places and promoting the two-way opening of the capital market. The picture shows shareholders watching the public board of the Shanghai-Hongkong Stock Exchange in the Qingdao Securities Exchange of Shandong Province.

··· **2014** ···

2014 年 11 月 19 日，浙江乌镇，为期三天的首届世界互联网大会在这里开幕。这是中国举办的规模最大、层次最高的互联网大会，也是世界互联网领域的高峰会议

On November 19, 2014, the first three-day World Internet Congress was held in Wuzhen, Zhejiang Province. This is the largest and highest-level Internet conference held by China, and also the world summit in the Internet field.

## ··· 2015 ···

2015 年 7 月 31 日，在国际奥委会第一百二十八次全会上，北京携手张家口获得 2022 年冬奥会举办权。图为民众在八达岭长城举行庆祝活动

On July 31, 2015, at the 128th IOC Plenary Session, Beijing joined hands with Zhangjiakou, Hebei Province to win the right to host the 2022 Winter Olympic Games. The picture shows people celebrating at the Badaling section of the Great Wall in Beijing.

··· 2015 ···

2015 年 8 月 29 日，2015 年北京国际田联世界田径锦标赛男子 4×100 米接力决赛在北京国家体育场"鸟巢"举行，中国队以 38 秒 01 的成绩获得银牌，这也是中国运动员在这一领域取得的最好成绩。图为当日中国队选手谢震业、苏炳添、张培萌和莫有雪（从左至右）赛后庆祝

On August 29, 2015, the men's 4×100m relay final of the 2015 IAAF World Champions was staged at the "Bird's Nest" (Beijing National Stadium), resulting in the Chinese team winning the silver medal in a time of 38.01 seconds. This was the best achievement Chinese athletes had made in this field. The picture shows Chinese athletes (left to right) Xie Zhenye, Su Bingtian, Zhang Peimeng and Mo Youxue after the race.

2015 年 9 月 3 日，中国人民抗日战争暨世界反法西斯战争胜利 70 周年纪念大会在北京隆重举行。图为抗战老兵乘车方队经过天安门广场

On September 3, 2015, the 70th Anniversary Congress of the Victory of the Chinese People's War of Resistance against Japan and the World War against Fascism was solemnly held in Beijing. The picture shows veterans of the anti-Japanese struggle passing through Tian'anmen Square in a motorcade.

## *2015*

2015 年 10 月 5 日，中国中医科学院研究员屠呦呦因在青蒿素研究中的杰出贡献，获得 2015 年诺贝尔生理学或医学奖，这是中国本土科学家首次获得诺贝尔自然科学奖项。图为 12 月 10 日，屠呦呦在诺贝尔奖颁奖仪式上领取奖章

On October 5, 2015, it was announced that Tu Youyou, a female researcher of the Chinese Academy of Traditional Chinese Medicine, had won the Nobel Prize in Physiology or Medicine in 2015 for his outstanding contribution to artemisinin research. It was the first time fort a Chinese native scientist to win the Nobel Prize in Natural Science. The picture shows Tu Youyou receiving her medal at the Nobel Prize Ceremony on December 10, 2015.

··· **2015** ···

随着移动支付的普及，出门不带钱包，随时随地移动支付逐渐成为一种国民消费习惯。图为2015年11月1日，浙江省杭州市，在杭州黄龙体育馆路边卖烤番薯的商贩们已采用二维码支付功能

With the surging popularity of mobile payments, it has become a national consumption habit to go out without wallet and pay anytime and anywhere by electronic means. The picture shows vendors selling baked sweet potatoes on the roadside of Huanglong Stadium in Hangzhou of Zhejiang Province had also adopted the two-dimensional code payment function on November 1, 2015.

**···2015···** 2015年12月8日，在江西省都昌县徐埠镇铭埠园特色农业开发公司示范基地，农民正在采摘瓜篓。近年来，江西省都昌县采取"公司＋贫困户"的方式着力推进特色种植精准扶贫，帮助贫困户从规模化经营、集约化生产中增加收入。"精准扶贫"的重要思想，是2013年11月习近平到湖南湘西考察时首次提出的

On December 8, 2015, at the demonstration base of the Mingbuyuan Special Agricultural Development Co., Xubu Town, Duchang County, Jiangxi Province, farmers were picking melons. In recent years, Duchang County of Jiangxi Province has taken the way of "business company + poor household" in effort to promote targeted poverty alleviation which helps increase their income from large-scale operation and intensive production. The important idea of targeted poverty alleviation was first put forward by Xi Jinping during his visit to Xiangxi of Hunan in November 2013.

··· *2015* ···

2015 年 12 月 27 日，十二届全国人大常委会第十八次会议在北京通过了关于修改《中华人民共和国人口与计划生育法》的决定，"全面两孩"政策将于 2016 年 1 月 1 日起施行。图为在安徽省合肥市一家"家有二宝体验馆"，育婴师在与一位有意向生二孩的母亲交流

On December 27, 2015, the 18th Session of the 12th NPC Standing Committee adopted a decision on Revising the Population and Family Planning Law in Beijing. The "two-children" policy would be implemented on January 1, 2016. The picture shows a second-child experience hall in Hefei, Anhui Province, where a nursery teacher talks with a mother intending to give birth to a second child.

2016年8月16日，我国成功发射世界首颗量子科学实验卫星"墨子号"。图为12月10日，在西藏阿里观测站，"墨子号"量子科学实验卫星过境，科研人员在做实验（合成照片）

On August 16, 2016, China successfully launched the world's first quantum science experimental satellite Mozi. The composite photos show the transit of the Mozi Quantum Science Experiment Satellite at the Ngari Observatory in Tibet with scientists carrying out experiments on December 10.

### ··· 2016 ···

2016 年 9 月 4 日至 5 日，以"构建创新、活力、联动、包容的世界经济"为主题的二十国集团领导人第十一次峰会在杭州举行。图为 9 月 4 日，杭州市，二十国集团峰会文艺晚会《最忆是杭州》

From September 4 to 5, 2016, the 11th Summit of the leaders of the Group of Twenty (G-20) was held in Hangzhou on the theme of "Building an Innovative, Vigorous, Linkage and Inclusive World Economy". The picture shows a scene of the G20 Literature and Art Gala *Most Memorable Is Hangzhou* on September 4, 2016.

2016年9月25日，具有我国自主知识产权的世界最大单口径巨型射电望远镜——500米口径球面射电望远镜（FAST）在贵州平塘落成启动。图为6月27日，FAST在满天繁星下呈现出的美丽景观

On September 25, 2016, the world's largest single-aperture giant radio telescope, the Five-Hundred-meter Aperture Spherical Radio Telescope (FAST), with China's independent intellectual property rights, was opened in Pingtang, Guizhou Province. The picture shows the beautiful scenery of FAST under the blinking stars.

··· **2016** ···

2016年11月1日，中国自主研制的新一代隐身战斗机歼-20首次公开亮相参加中国珠海国际航展。这是中国自主研制的新一代隐身战斗机首次公开亮相。图为飞行中的歼-20

On November 1, 2016, the new-generation stealth fighter J-20 independently developed by China made its first public appearance at the Zhuhai International Air Show.

2016 年 11 月 5 日，在美国拉斯维加斯举行的 WBO（世界拳击组织）蝇量级金腰带争夺战中，中国职业拳手邹市明首次夺得 WBO 蝇量级世界拳王金腰带。图为邹市明（中）庆祝胜利

On November 5, 2016, Chinese professional boxer Zou Shiming won the WBO (World Boxing Organization) flyweight world title for the first time in Las Vegas. The picture shows Zou (middle) celebrating his victory.

··· 2017 ···

2017 年 3 月 28 日，中共中央、国务院发出通知，决定设立河北雄安新区。这是继深圳经济特区和上海浦东新区之后又一具有全国意义的新区

On March 28, 2017, the CPC Central Committee and the State Council issued a circular deciding to establish the Xiongan New Area in Hebei Province. This is another new area of national significance after the Shenzhen Special Economic Zone in southern China, and the Shanghai Pudong New Area.

**···2017···**

2017 年 5 月 5 日，我国自主研制的首款 C919 大型客机首飞成功。图为 11 月 10 日，我国自主研制的 C919 大型客机在上海浦东国际机场起飞

On May 5, 2017, the large C919 passenger airliner independently developed by China made its first successful flight. The picture shows the take-off of C919 at the Shanghai Pudong International Airport on November 10.

··· **2017** ···

2017 年 5 月 14 日至 15 日，第一届"一带一路"国际合作高峰论坛在北京举行。此次高峰论坛主题为"加强国际合作，共建'一带一路'，实现共赢发展"。高峰论坛至今已成功举办两届。图为首届高峰论坛开幕前夕，北京奥林匹克公园大道被装点得花团锦簇

From May 14 to 15, 2017, the first Belt and Road Forum for International Cooperation was held in Beijing. The theme of this summit forum is "strengthening international cooperation and co-building the Belt and Road for win-win development". The Summit Forum has been successfully held for two sessions so far. Picture shows the Beijing Olympic Park Avenue decorated with flowers on the eve of the opening of the First Summit Forum.

··· **2017** ···

2017 年 7 月 1 日，习近平出席在香港举行的《深化粤港澳合作 推进大湾区建设框架协议》签署仪式。建设粤港澳大湾区成为国家战略。图为 2017 年 12 月 12 日晚上，粤港澳大湾区城市旅游联合会在广东珠海正式成立

On July 1, 2017, President Xi Jinping attended the signing ceremony of the Framework Agreement on Deepening Guangdong-Hong Kong-Macao Cooperation in the Development of the Greater Bay Area held in Hong Kong. Building the Greater Bay Area of Guangdong, Hong Kong and Macao has become a national strategy. The picture shows the founding of the Zhuhai-Hong Kong-Macao Dawan District Urban Tourism Federation on the evening of December 12, 2017 in Zhuhai.

**··· 2017 ···**

2017 年 9 月 3 日至 5 日，金砖国家领导人第九次会晤在福建厦门举行。图为 9 月 5 日拍摄的厦门国际会议中心

From September 3 to 5, 2017, the ninth BRICS Summit was held in Xiamen, Fujian Province. The picture shows the Xiamen International Conference Center on September 5.

2017 年 10 月 18 日至 24 日，中国共产党第十九次全国代表大会举行。大会通过关于《中国共产党章程（修正案）》的决议

The 19th National Congress of the CPC held in Beijing from October 18 to 24, 2017 adopted the Resolution on Amendment to CPC Constitution.

**··· 2017 ···**

2017 年，华为智能手机全年发货 1.53 亿台，在中国市场份额突破 20%，全球份额突破 10%，稳居全球前三。华为、中车等中国高科技企业不断开辟国际市场，把"中国智慧"带给世界。图为在阿根廷首都布宜诺斯艾利斯，顾客（中）购买到在当地发售的首部华为 Y6 智能手机

In 2017, Huawei shipped 153 million smartphones a year, achieving a market share of more than 20% in China and 10% in the world, ranking among the top three in the world. China's high-tech enterprises, such as Huawei and CRRC, continue to open up international markets and bring "Chinese wisdom" to the world. The picture shows the first Huawei Y6 smartphone being sold to customers in Buenos Aires, Argentina.

··· *2018* ···

2018 年年初，经党中央批准、国务院批复，自 2018 年起，将每年农历秋分设立为中国农民丰收节，这是第一个在国家层面为农民设立的节日。图为首个中国农民丰收节，拉萨两名藏族农民在田间聊天

At the beginning of 2018, with the approval of the CPC Central Committee and the State Council, the autumn equinox of the lunar calendar was established as a harvest festival for Chinese farmers, which is the first festival set up for farmers at the national level. Picture shows two Tibetan farmers in Lhasa chatting in the fields during the event.

## ··· *2018* ···

2018 年 9 月 3 日至 4 日，中非合作论坛北京峰会举行。会议通过《关于构建更加紧密的中非命运共同体的北京宣言》和《中非合作论坛——北京行动计划（2019—2021 年）》。图为中非合作论坛开幕式在北京人民大会堂举行

From September 3 to 4, 2018, the Beijing Summit of the Forum on China-Africa Cooperation was held. It adopted the Beijing Declaration - Toward an Even Stronger China-Africa Community with a Shared Future and the Beijing Action Plan of the Forum on China-Africa Cooperation (2019-2021). The picture shows the grand opening of the event in the Great Hall of the People.

### ··· *2018* ···

2018 年 10 月 23 日，港珠澳大桥开通仪
式在广东省珠海市举行。港珠澳大桥是
"一国两制"框架下粤港澳三地首次合
作建设的大型跨海交通工程，也是世界
上最长的跨海大桥工程。图为 7 月 17 日
拍摄的港珠澳大桥

On October 23, 2018, the opening ceremony
of the Hong Kong-Zhuhai-Macao Bridge was
held in Zhuhai City, Guangdong Province.
The Hong Kong-Zhuhai-Macao Bridge is
the first large-scale cross-sea traffic project
constructed by the three southern areas
under the framework of "one country, two
systems", and it is also the longest cross-sea
bridge project in the world. The picture shows
the bridge in operation on July 17, 2018.

··· **2018** ···

2018 年 11 月 5 日至 10 日，首届中国国际进口博览会在上海国家会展中心举行。图为中国馆展示的骨科手术机器人

From November 5 to 10, 2018, the first China International Import Exposition was held in the Shanghai National Convention and Exhibition Center. The picture shows an orthopedic surgical robot on display in the Chinese Pavilion.

··· *2018* ···

2018 年 11 月 9 日，国家综合性消防救援队伍授旗仪式在北京人民大会堂举行。综合性消防救援队伍由国家应急管理部管理，是由公安消防部队、武警森林部队退出现役，成建制划归应急管理部后组建成立国家综合性消防救援队伍。图为仪仗队员护卫着中国消防救援队队旗正步行进

On November 9, 2018, the flag-giving ceremony of the National Comprehensive Fire Rescue Team was held in the Great Hall of the People in Beijing. The team, subject to management by the Ministry of Emergency Management of the State Council, is formed by members of the former Public Security Fire-fighting Forces and Armed Police Forest Forces. The picture shows a guard of honor escorting the flag of the Chinese Fire Rescue Team.

···**2019**···

2019 年 1 月 11 日，北京市级行政中心正式迁入北京城市副中心。图为当日拍摄的新揭牌的北京市人民政府办公楼

On January 11, 2019, the administrative center at the Beijing municipal level officially moved into the Subsidiary Center of Beijing. The picture shows the newly unveiled office building of the Beijing Municipal People's Government.

··· *2019* ···

2019 年 1 月 23 日，国产首个市域动车组在温州轨道交通 S1 线上线运营。图为首批进站的市民纷纷拿起手机拍照留念

On January 23, 2019, China's first municipal electrical multiple unit (EMU) service began operating on line S1 of the Wenzhou Rail Transit. The picture shows the first batch of inbound citizens taking pictures as a souvenir.

··· *2019* ···

2019 年 2 月 15 日，中国国家航天局、中国科学院和国际天文学联合会联合召开新闻发布会，向全世界发布"嫦娥四号"着陆区域月球地理实体的命名。这也标志着"嫦娥四号"任务取得的成果得到了国际认可

On February 15, 2019, the National Space Administration of China, the Chinese Academy of Sciences and the International Astronomical Federation jointly held a press conference to announce to the world the naming of the lunar geographic entity in Chang'e-4 lunar module landing area. This also marked international recognition of the Chang'e-4 mission.

··· **2019** ···

2019 年 2 月 5 日，中国科幻电影《流浪地球》上映。凭借良好的口碑，该电影在海内外电影市场的激烈竞争中脱颖而出，获得了骄人的票房成绩。《纽约时报》评述道：《流浪地球》标志中国电影新时代到来，也是中国科幻片元年的开启。图为科幻电影《流浪地球》定档发布会合影

On February 5, 2019, the Chinese science fiction film *The Wandering Earth* was released. With good reputation, the film stands out in the fierce competition in the domestic and foreign film market, and has achieved remarkable box office results. The *New York Times* comments that *The Wandering Earth* marks the arrival of a new era of Chinese film and the beginning of the first year of Chinese science fiction. The picture shows the filing conference of the sci-fi film *The Wandering Earth*.

# ··· *2019* ···

2019 年 4 月 29 日，北京世界园艺博览会在北京市延庆区举行。北京世界园艺博览会是中国承办过的最高级别的世界园艺博览会之一，是继云南昆明后第二个获得国际园艺生产者协会批准及国际展览局认证授权举办的 A1 级国际园艺博览会。图为北京世园会园区夜景

On April 29, 2019, the World Horticultural Exposition Park was held in Yanqing District, Beijing, lasting 162 days. The Beijing Exposition is one of the highest-level horticultural expositions hosted by China, and is the second level of International Horticultural Exposition after the one in Kunming, Yunnan Province, which has been approved by the International Horticultural Producers Association and authorized by the International Exhibition Bureau. The picture shows a night view of the Beijing World Garden Expo Park taken by UAV.

# 结束语

时光如水，日月如梭。但那些伟大的历史瞬间，总是会被人们铭记。在 2017 年 10 月 18 日，习近平总书记在中国共产党第十九次全国代表大会上指出：不忘初心，方得始终。中国共产党人的初心和使命，就是为中国人民谋幸福，为中华民族谋复兴。这个初心和使命是激励中国共产党人不断前进的根本动力。全党同志一定要永远与人民同呼吸、共命运、心连心，永远把人民对美好生活的向往作为奋斗目标，以永不懈怠的精神状态和一往无前的奋斗姿态，继续朝着实现中华民族伟大复兴的宏伟目标奋勇前进。

抚今追昔，挖掘峥嵘历史背后那些鲜为人知的往事，既是对历史的回望，也告诫我们要珍惜来之不易的美好生活，更是对未来美好的憧憬。

70 年来，在党的正确领导下，在中国人民及海内外华人同胞的共同努力下，新中国取得了举世瞩目的成就，民族独立、人民解放、国家富强、百姓安居乐业。

"与国同梦"是坚持，是信仰，是久久不变的情怀。中华民族伟大复兴的宏伟誓愿，正在世界的东方回响。同心同德，同向同行。美好生活，正在每一个中国人手中创造。

# CONCLUDING REMARKS

Of the events occurring in history, great ones are passed down in history from generation to generation. On October 18, 2017, Xi Jinping, General Secretary of the CPC Central Committee, pointed out at the 19th National Party Congress:"Never forget why you started, and you can accomplish your mission. The original aspiration and the mission of Chinese Communists is to seek happiness for the Chinese people and rejuvenation for the Chinese nation. This original aspiration, this mission, is what inspires Chinese Communists to advance. In our Party, each and every one of us must always breathe the same breath as the people, share the same future, and stay truly connected to them. The aspirations of the people to live a better life must always be the focus of our efforts. We must keep on striving with endless energy toward the great goal of national rejuvenation."

Looking back on the past and striving to dig out the little-known past events is not only to look back on history, but is also a reminder to us to cherish the hard-won good life and also consider our vision of the future.

The PRC, under the correct leadership of the CPC and with the joint efforts of the Chinese people and their compatriots at home and abroad, have, since the founding of New China in 1949, made remarkable achievements, winning national independence, people's total liberation and great national prosperity.

"Dreaming with the nation" means persistence, belief and lasting emotion. The grand pledge for the great rejuvenation of the Chinese nation is echoing in the East of the world. With one mind, the whole nation is working hard to create a better life! As these pictures show, it has been a wonderful journey so far.

**70 Years of the People's Republic**

**Written by Jiang Yongqing**
**Translated by Zhong Lisha**

**Planning Editor:** Yu Jiutao
**Managing Editor:** Fang Yunzhong
**Editor:** Liu Xiaoxue
**English Editor:** Ye Shujun
**English Language Consultant:** Wang Guozhen, Chen Xu

China Pictorial Press

33 Chegongzhuang West Road, Haidian District, Beijing, 100048, China

First Printed in September 2019

## 图片提供：

**人民画报社、新华通讯社、解放军报社、视觉中国、中国新闻社、中国图片集团**

阿兰·诺格、安佑忠、保罗·斯莱德、贝特曼·科尔维斯、布鲁塞·达莱、常潇潇、陈飞、陈捷、陈思禹、陈小波、纯德摄、戴纪明、丁汀、董希文、方爱玲、费茂华、傅建斌、弗兰克·菲施贝克、戈春江、格桑达瓦、管绍熙、郭建设、郭修生、郝纯一、何宗跃、侯建森、胡志强、黄一鸣、蒋超、蒋铎、觉果、鞠焕宗、拉比·穆格拉比、李怀德、李然、李生南、李涛、李向新、李鑫、李学增、李一方、李治元、廖新刚、刘大伟、刘非、刘宏鹏、刘建生、刘廷芳、刘宇、刘玉生、马俊峰、马宁、米立公、钮一新、裴鑫、帕斯卡尔·勒塞格格雷坦、普布扎西、戚恒、钱捍、钱晓虎、孙凯芳、索向鲁、谭志强、唐禹民、王安、王辰增、王呈选、王敬德、王丽莉、王文澜、王文扬、王永建、王子瑾、魏志阳、翁乃强、吴良荣、吴吕明、吴鹏飞、吴雍、夏道陵、熊汝清、徐义根、雪印、杨焕敏、杨俊江、杨磊、杨世尧、杨卫华、殷刚、游云谷、于文国、袁蒙、原瑞伦、曾曙生、查春明、张爱林、张铖、张春雷、张端、张国俊、张海鹏、张文礼、张郓、张由琼、张兆增、赵承顺、郑书福、周浩、周华、周家国、周文杰、周盈盈、朱建国、朱鹏

（按姓氏拼音排序）

## Photos contributed by CFB, Xinhua News, PLA Daily, VCG, CNS, CIG

Photos courtesy of Alain Nogues, An Youzhong, Paul Slade, Betman Colvis, Bruce Dale, Chang Xiaoxiao, Chen Fei, Chen Jie, Chen Siyu, Chen Xiaobo, Chun Denie, Dai Jiming, Ding Ting, Dong Xiwen, Fang Ailing, Fei Maohua, Fu Jianbin, Frank Fischbeck, Ge Chunjiang, Gesandawa, Guan Shaoxi, Guo Jianshe, Guo Xiusheng, Hao Chunyi, He Zongyue, Hou Jiansen, Hu Zhiqiang, Huang Yiming, Jiang Chao, Jiang Duo, Jue Guo, Ju Huanzhong, Rabbi Mugrabi, Li Huaide, Li Ran, Li Shengnan, Li Tao, Li Xiangxin, Li Xuezeng, Li Yifang, Li Zhiyuan, Liao Xingang, Liu Dawei, Liu Fei, Liu Hongpeng, Liu Jiansheng, Liu Tingfang, Liu Yu, Liu Yusheng, Ma Junfeng, Ma Ning, Mi Ligong, Niu Yixin, Pei Xin, Pascal Lesser Gretan, Pubzasi, Qi Heng, Qian Han, Qian Xiaohu, Sun Kaifang, Suo Xianglu, Tan Zhiqiang, Tang Yumin, Wang An, Wang Chenzeng, Wang Chengxuan, Wang Jingde, Wang Lili, Wang Wenlan, Wang Wenyang, Wang Yongjian, Wang Zijin, Wei Zhiyang, Weng Naiqiang, Wu Liangrong, Wu Lyuming, Wu Pengfei, Wu Yong, Xia Daoling, Xiong Ruqing, Xu Yigen, Xue Yin, Yang Huanmin, Yang Junjiang, Yang Lei, Yang Shiyao, Yang Weihua, Yin Gang, You Yungu, Yu Wenguo, Yuan Meng, Yuan Ruilun, Zeng Shusheng, Zha Chunming, Zhang Ailin, Zhang Rong, Zhang Chunlei, Zhang Duan, Zhang Guojun, Zhang Haipeng, Zhang Wenli, Zhang Xun, Zhang Youqiong, Zhang Yuqiong, Zhang Zhaozeng, Zhao Chengshun, Zheng Shufu, Zhou Hao, Zhou Hua, Zhou Jiaguo, Zhou Wenjie, Zhou Yingying, Zhu Jianguo and Zhu Peng

(Arranged in alphabetical order of surnames)